The OJ Simpson Murder Case

The OJ Simpson Murder Case

Voices of True Crime

Book 1

Alan R. Warren

Copyright

The O.J. Simpson Case
True Crimes Interviews Series: Volume 1
Written by Alan R. Warren
Published by House of Mystery

Copyright @ 2022 by Alan R. Warren

Cover design, formatting, layout, and editing by Evening Sky Publishing Services

Published in United States of America
ISBN (eBook): 978-1-989980-74-3
ISBN (Paperback): 978-1-989980-75-0

Contents

Introduction   vii

1. O.J. Simpson   1
2. Murders of Nicole Brown Simpson
   and Ron Goldman   7
3. The Prosecution   23
   Interview with Marcia Clark
4. For the Defense   41
   Interview with F. Lee Bailey
5. The Survivors   77
   Interview with Kim Goldman
6. Who Killed Nicole?   103
   Interview with Norman Pardo
7. Las Vegas Arrest   131
   Interview with Andy Caldwell

References   159
About the Author   167
Also in The House of Mystery
Interview Series   169

Introduction

The *House of Mystery Radio Show* has been on the air for ten years now, broadcasting in over a dozen cities in the United States, including KKNW 1150 A.M. Seattle/Tacoma, KCAA 106.5 F.M. Los Angeles/102.3 F.M. Riverside/1050 A.M. Palm Springs. I started the show to find as much information on the world's mysteries in crime, science, religion, history, paranormal, and more. Like most people, I have heard stories and rumors and read books or watched documentaries on television, but I would seldom hear one direct answer to a question. Throughout my time recording interviews, I sought out people who had themselves researched a subject enough to have written a book or created a documentary, or even people involved in the event or topic that would have first-hand knowledge.

In most cases, the strange thing was that there was a popular or mainstream idea about what happened; one reported at the time of the event, but then there was an alternative idea. Most writers who had books or shows that did well often disagreed with the current theory and accused the media of faking the story and hiding the truth from everyone. An example would be "Who shot JFK?" Different government agencies and news media have reported a well-known theory that most people in America have come to accept as the truth. But since the original Warren Report on JFK's assassination, there have been hundreds of theories promoted by many authors and lots of research completed.

The *House of Mystery Interview Series* is a series of books that contain transcriptions of the very best interviews we've had on several topics. So far, seven books have been published covering the Jack the Ripper case, the JFK assassination, the Zodiac Killer, mysterious celebrity deaths, conspiracy theories, paranormal and the occult, and the D.B. Cooper hijacking. You will find the books in the "Also in The House of Mystery

Interviews Series" section of this book and on my website.

A substantial number of our interviews revolve around true crime. So, we created this sub-series, *Voices of True Crime*. Like the other Interviews series, we review the most accepted explanation of the case. Then, we follow up with each theory presented during our interviews with the person or people reporting them. Each book lays out the case details and then follows up with what we've learned from each guest.

Like the others in the *House of Mystery Radio Show Interviews Series,* this book does not attempt to solve the case but only reviews it. There will be no committed answer at the end of the book. We aim to concisely review the extraordinary things we learned during the show's interviews. It is an excellent reference for researchers and a good overview for people who don't know the topic well. Similar to the other volumes in this series, only the highlights of each interview will be included. All these interviews and more are available to listen to on my website: www. alanrwarren.com/hom-podcast-episodes.

～

Over the last century, there have been plenty of trials called "The Trial of the Century," but of all mentioned, the O.J. Simpson case rose well above the rest. Not only because the accused murderer was a high-profile athlete and celebrity and because of the brutality of the murders, but more because of how far the media had advanced. By the mid-1990s, the internet had begun its revolution. Cell phones started becoming regular things people owned, and satellites brought hundreds of television channels into our homes.

Once the police determined probable cause for them to arrest O.J. Simpson and charge him with two murders, the chase was on. Literally. Simpson's lawyer, Robert Shapiro, made an agreement with police for Simpson to turn himself in by noon on June 17th. While more than a thousand journalists surrounded the police station to get pictures of Simpson being arrested, he would never show up. Instead, Simpson disappeared. By 2 p.m. that afternoon, police declared Simpson a fugitive and issued a warrant for his arrest.

At 5 p.m. that same afternoon, Simpson's lawyer Shapiro made a public appeal on television for Simpson to turn himself in. He then read a suicide note that Simpson had written, leading to panic amongst his family and friends. The search was on involving all levels of law enforcement and almost every citizen in Los Angeles. Joining the police in the quest to find O.J. was all the news media, who were using every helicopter at their disposal. In all history, this must have been the first search for a suspect that included this many people in the city while being watched live on television.

Simpson had last been seen with his good friend Al Cowling who drove a white Ford Bronco. The Bronco had been on all the news reports, so everyone in the city was looking for it. Around 6:30 that same evening, another driver driving on the I-5 called 911 to report seeing O.J. and Al Cowling heading North. Police tracked Simpson's cell phone from his calls until finally, officer Ruth Dixon spotted Cowling's white Bronco going North on Interstate 405.

Dixon caught up with the Bronco and drove parallel with them when Cowling opened his window to let her know that O.J. was in the back of the vehicle holding a gun to his own head, threatening to shoot himself. The officer slowed down and started following them instead. Soon, as many as twenty other police cars would follow Simpson and Cowling on the highway. They were all going at a slow speed of about 35 miles per hour. It wouldn't be long before every news helicopter had its cameras on the slow-speed chase and was televised worldwide. There was an estimated 95 million viewers in the U.S. alone. All the streets and overpasses were filled with spectators; surprisingly, many of them had signs telling him to run. As the white Bronco drove by, groups shouted things like "Go, O.J. Go!"

Simpson, through Cowling, told detectives that he wouldn't surrender until he could speak with his mother in person. Law enforcement let the two of them drive to Simpson's Brentwood home, arriving around 8 p.m. Simpson was allowed to go in and be with his mother for about an hour while at least 25 SWAT officers surrounded the house and waited. Simpson surrendered as soon as his lawyer, Shapiro, arrived. Both Simpson and Cowlings were arrested.

In Cowling's Bronco, police found about $8,000. In a case, they found a .357 Magnum gun, loaded, Simpson's passport, a disguise kit composed of a fake mustache and goatee, and a spare set of clothing. After this day, how could this not end up being the trial of the century?

Chapter 1
O.J. Simpson

If there has ever been a name we have all heard of, at times even too much, it's O.J. Simpson. The man's superstar NFL football career was overshadowed by his televised trial for the murder of his former wife Nicole Brown-Simpson and Ronald Goldman. What happens when a public figure who is so popular gets accused of murder? Do his fans stay behind him even if he turns out guilty? That's a rather complex question to answer, and I'm not sure it can be, but it's something worth thinking about when going through this book. How much evidence or facts can one ignore before they come to terms with their idol's guilt?

Simpson was raised in the housing projects in San Francisco in the Potrero Hill neighborhood with his parents, who both worked average jobs. Consequently, it wasn't too much of a surprise that his younger years were full of minor arrests from his time being a part of a street gang, the "Persian Warriors." Simpson eventually ended up in the San Francisco Guidance Center for petty crimes.

After meeting baseball legend Willie Mays, Simpson decided to straighten out his life. He married childhood sweetheart Marguerite Whitley, and they had two children. After graduation, Simpson enrolled in City College of San Francisco, where he played college football. After winning the Prune Bowl, universities pursued him to transfer to their school and play for their team. His two-year college football record was impressive, and he was picked by the NFL's Buffalo Bills football team in the 1969 draft for what was then the largest contract in professional football history at $650,000.

In the summer of 1977, after meeting a waitress, Nicole Brown, O.J. Simpson's life completely changed. He separated from his wife, one of his daughters drowned, and he was traded to the San Francisco 49ers, where he would play his final two seasons of professional football. Simpson was later inducted into the Pro Football Hall of Fame for his record-breaking career in 1985. That same year, he married Nicole Brown, and they had their first child, Sydney Brook Simpson.

In May 1989, the public saw a possible forecast of things to come after O.J. was convicted for spousal abuse. He was sentenced to two years probation, 120 hours of community service, and a $450 fine. He also had to pay a $500 fee to attend the Sojourn Women's Program, where he attended battery counselling. Their marriage only lasted seven years when they divorced in February 1992. During the following two years, they were still very involved with each other and, at times, appeared to be romantically involved again.

In 1986, Jimmie Lee Simpson, O.J.'s dad, died

of AIDS. Jimmy was a popular drag queen who performed around the city of San Francisco for years. He told his family he was gay a few years before his death. Since his parents were divorced in 1952, O.J. lived with his mother, and his father never played a significant role in his day-to-day life.

After Simpson retired from professional football, he focused on his acting career, which actually started before he played professional football. He starred in the pilot episode of the popular television series *Medical Center* in 1969, starring Chad Everett. Riding on the wave of his success and popularity, Simpson starred in many television movies such as *The Towering Inferno, Capricorn One,* and even the miniseries *Roots.* He is best known for being in the comedy movie trio *The Naked Gun* and his Hertz Rent-A-Car television commercial. Hertz claimed their business increased by 50% within the first moments of O.J. being their spokesman.

By 1993, Simpson got a contract to star in a two-hour movie pilot and television series for Warner Brothers called *Frogmen,* to be aired in 1994. But after he was arrested in June of 1994, NBC canceled the series, which never aired. In the movie and series, Simpson was to play a U.S.

Navy Seal, and it was reported that he starred in a scene where he held a knife to a woman's throat. The scene was too close to the murder of Nicole Brown-Simpson, and the network didn't want to air it. It cost them an estimated $14 million in losses because they felt they could never release it on home video.

Chapter 2
Murders of Nicole Brown Simpson and Ron Goldman

On June 12, 1994, the school year was close to wrapping up, and the excitement for summer vacation spread among the kids in class. This evening, the Paul Revere Middle School was having a dance recital, and Sydney Simpson was performing in it. She was excited to see both her parents show up to watch her, O.J. Simpson and Nicole Brown-Simpson. Her parents had divorced recently, and she was living with her mother, so any chance to see her father, especially together with her mother, was exciting for her. But after the dance recital was over, her mother, grandmother, and a few other family members all went out to celebrate with a nice dinner. Mezzaluna had become a regular spot for them to go as they loved the light atmosphere and great food. One of the waitpeople, Ron Goldman, had become a good friend with Nicole over the last few months as he was a waiter there and served the family often.

When they arrived at the restaurant, Sydney quickly realized that her father wasn't joining them. She never said anything to her mother because this kind of thing wasn't unusual, but she would miss him. They were usually served by a friend of Nicole's, Ron Goldman. He was great with the kids and knew the family well. But on this night, his section was already full, so he wouldn't be their waiter that night.

After dinner, the family stopped at a local Ben & Jerry's for some ice cream before heading home for the night. Once the family got home and the kids went to bed, Nicole's mother realized that she didn't have her glasses with her, so she decided to contact the restaurant to see if she could have left them there. The manager found them, put them in an envelope, and told her they would be there with her name on the envelope anytime she wanted to pick them up.

Ron Goldman overheard the conversation, grabbed the envelope, and told the manager he could drop them off at Nicole's house because it was just a few blocks from where he was going. When he got off work at about 10 p.m. that night, he headed out to drop off the glasses and then get home to change before going out.

Meanwhile, across town, after O.J. left the recital, he went and picked up Kato Kaelin, a friend who had been living in Simpson's guest house. According to Simpson, the two of them went to McDonald's to eat. Later, it was reported by Cindy Adams at the *New York Post* that they had actually gone to a Burger King because they wanted to buy some crystal meth and knew that they could buy it there. The report also had the drug dealer by the name of J.R. admitting that he did sell them drugs that night at Burger King.

After a couple of Nicole's neighbors found her dog out on the street, barking and covered in blood, they took it home to care for it before walking it back home. When they arrived just outside of Nicole's place, the dog stopped. The couple decided to step onto the property, hopefully, to get the dog to follow them, when they noticed Brown's body lying on the ground. They quickly called the police, who would also find Ron Goldman's body.

When police arrived at Brown's condominium, they found the front door was wide open, but there were no signs of breaking or entering. Nicole's body was lying face down at the bottom of the stairwell that led to the front door. The walk that led to the stairs where she was found was covered in blood, but Nicole's feet were bare, dry, and clean. She had been stabbed in the head and neck and had some defensive wounds on her hands.

A footprint on the back of her clothing made detectives believe that the killer stood on her back while pulling her head back by her hair. Then, her throat was slit so deep that her head was almost removed from her body. The cause of death was the severing of her carotid artery. Detectives believe she was the intended target and probably the first to have been killed.

Police found Ron Goldman's body beside a

tree beside the property fence. He was also stabbed several times throughout his body, including the neck but with very few defensive cuts on his hands or arms, indicating there probably wasn't much of a fight before he was killed. The city coroner stated that Goldman was probably held by the throat by one of the killer's hands while he was stabbed by the other.

Evidence found at the murder scene included a blue knit cap, an extra-large left-handed men's Aris Isotoner leather glove, and the envelope that contained the glasses Nicole's mother had left at the restaurant. This led detectives to believe that Goldman was probably on his way to drop off the glasses and saw Nicole being attacked by the killer. The killer turned his attack toward Goldman to ensure that there were no living witnesses.

Small drops of blood along the walkway went right through the back gate, which seemed to run alongside some bloody shoe prints left by the killer. Detectives believed that the drops of blood probably came from the left hand of the killer, who must have been cut during the struggles with both victims.

On June 13, Simpson was scheduled to play in a golf tournament in Chicago for the Hertz Rent-a-car company as he was their spokesman. He had a flight booked on the same night as the murders, which was scheduled to leave Los Angeles at 11:45 p.m. Simpson's limo ride to take him to the airport arrived around 10:30 that night, and the driver started to buzz Simpson's house at 10:40, but he got no answer. The driver later testified that Simpson's house was completely dark, but eventually, he saw a man the same size as Simpson enter the house through the front driveway. Soon after that, the house lights all came on. Shortly after that, Kato Kaelin noticed the limo waiting outside the fence, so he went out and let him in. Simpson finally came out, got into the limo, and headed to the airport. Later, the driver also testified to loading three bags of luggage into the car and that Simpson also had a bag with him that he didn't let the driver place in the trunk with the other bags. The airport baggage handler only checked in three bags for Simpson for that flight.

A key witness for detectives was someone at the airport who claimed to have seen Simpson throwing away things from that bag into the garbage can at the airport. That witness would never testify in court, but detectives were positive this was where Simpson disposed of key evidence such as his bloody clothes, shoes, and the murder weapon.

Another part of the case that garnered lots of debate was Simpson's cut hand. The pilot and a passenger on the same flight to Chicago with Simpson testified that he had no cut on his hand. Simpson claimed to have cut his hand in his hotel room when he heard about Nicole's murder when he put his glass too hard on the table, and it broke. Detectives found the broken glass and a bedsheet with blood on it from his hotel in Chicago. The hotel manager also testified that Simpson had asked him for a band-aid for a cut he had on his finger.

On June 13th, detectives picked Simpson up at his home and took him in for questioning surrounding the death of Brown and Goldman. They took note of the cut on his finger on his left hand, which was also where they figured the killer had left the drops of blood on the walkway. Simpson told detectives that he had cut his finger in the hotel room in Chicago, but when they informed him that they had also found blood in his car, he said that he had made a mistake. And that he had actually cut his hand on June 12th, but he couldn't remember how he cut it.

The next day Simpson hired Robert Shapiro,

who started to put together what would later be called the "Dream Team" of lawyers to be prepared for any arrest. When the DNA of the blood found at the crime scene came back as a match to Simpson, the District Attorney recommended Simpson be arrested and charged with the two counts of murder. Detectives told his lawyer Shapiro, and they gave Simpson one day to turn himself into authorities.

Simpson took the time he had to update his will and write three letters: one was addressed to his mother, one to his kids, and the other to the public. Everyone waited for Simpson and his lawyer to arrive at the police precinct, but he never did. After an hour, the police chief made an official statement informing the public that a warrant had been issued for Simpson for the murders of Brown and Goldman.

The police arrived at Simpson's residence only to find him and his friend Al Cowlings missing. By 5 p.m. that day, Shapiro read aloud the letter that Simpson had left for the public,

"First, everyone understands I had nothing to do with Nicole's murder. I can't go on. Don't feel sorry for me. I have had a great life and great friends. Please think of the real O.J. and not this lost person."

After Shapiro finished reading the letter, he pleaded for Simpson to turn himself in. This plea would lead to the most famous slow-speed car chase in history and all televised worldwide.

Now that the world was caught up in the case drama, the media had to try and continue the momentum. When the trial started, many people had already become invested in the case, but with all dramatic things, the media wanted more. They would follow anyone involved in the case—trying to get pictures or anything that might interest viewers.

Marcia Clark, the prosecutor, was followed and talked about by commentators daily. "She changed her hairstyle. What do you think?" would be the question on the air. Whenever Clark was spotted in public, people would tell her to change her outfit, wear more tailored skirts, or they loved her new hairstyle or thought it was awful. It didn't stop there. Deep media searches revealed pictures of Clark topless on the beach years before the trial. Anything and everything they could find was all open territory to them.

Witnesses like the limo driver who drove Simpson to the airport the evening of the murders were approached. He was offered $100,000 to tell his story to the press but refused because he wouldn't be called to testify if he did say anything to anyone in public. Other witnesses seemed to love the attention and try to take advantage of their new-found fame. Kato Kaelin would take any offer he had and ended up being on more television shows than any other witness, enough to become a household name.

Once Judge Ito was assigned to the case, one of the first significant decisions he faced was whether to let the media cameras into the courtroom during the trial. Ito decided to allow the trial to be televised, which really foreshadowed how the rest of the trial would play out. With well over 2,000 news outlets broadcasting from the trial, how could the trial and all of its participants not be influenced by it? Even well-established news magazines such as *Time* and *Newsweek* made the trial not only something they reported on, but it also became the lead story on their covers editions. The attention was worldwide. When Russian President Boris Yeltsin met U.S. President Bill Clinton at their summit, the first question that he asked Clinton was if he thought O.J. did it.

The trial started on January 24, 1995, and lasted one hundred and thirty-four days. One of the first major criticisms of the trial was the decision of the District Attorney to hold the trial in downtown Los Angeles instead of Santa Monica, where the murders happened. Reports surfaced that having the trial there would mean that the jury pool to draw from would be predominantly African American and not good for the prosecution. This was mainly because of the Rodney King decision that happened just a couple of years before, when four police officers were acquitted of assault and excessive force charges during the arrest and beating of Rodney King.

That event started on the early morning hours of a Sunday in March 1991, when King, along with two friends, was driving west on Interstate 210 in the San Fernando Valley on their way home from watching a basketball game at a friend's. Two California Highway Patrol officers noticed them speeding by at a high rate of speed. The two patrol officers chased King with their lights and sirens blaring, but King refused to pull over. He knew he was drinking and would test above the legal limit. Not only that, but he did not want to lose his license. He was on parole at this time and figured that he'd end up in jail.

It wasn't long before several other officers joined the pursuit and a helicopter. Only a short time later, officers cornered King and stopped him. Highway Patrol officer Tim Singer yelled for the three occupants to exit the vehicle and lay face down on the ground with their hands raised above their heads. Both passengers got out of the car and lay on the ground as asked, but both were hit and kicked while they lay there. King remained in the car, doing nothing. Eventually, King got out of the car but wasn't complying with the officer's orders. Instead, he waved his hands at the helicopter flying above him and laughed.

King, then with both hands, grabbed his behind, which Highway Patrol officer Melanie Singer thought he was reaching for a weapon, so she drew her gun and yelled at King to get on the ground. Just before she could arrest King, the LAPD officer in charge at the scene told her to back down, put her weapon back in her holster, and that they would be taking control of the situation.

Koon, the LAPD officer in charge, told his men to arrest and handcuff King by using a police technique called a "swarm," where several officers grab a suspect simultaneously to confuse them and to allow them to subdue them quickly with less of a chance of hurting anybody. All four officers later stated that King resisted their attempts to arrest him, and King would later deny this. Officers even said that because King acted so wild, they figured he was on PCP, but later blood tests proved that he wasn't.

Around this time, George Holliday heard the commotion outside his apartment building. When he looked out the window and saw all the police with their lights flashing, he grabbed his camcorder and started filming the incident. The video showed the officers tasering King, and when he got up to try and run away, the officers at the scene would hit him several times with batons. King kept trying to stand up, so the officers started hitting him on his joint areas, such as the wrist, knees, and ankles. By the time they finally got King under control, and in cuffs, eight officers were swarming him, all of them hitting him with their batons or kicking him.

George Holliday called the LAPD headquarters two days after King's arrest and told them that he had videotaped the whole arrest and wanted to know if they wanted a copy of it or to watch it, but they were not interested in it at all. After police turned Holliday down for his video, he decided to go to KTLA in Los Angeles. This video was gold for them, and it became something that was shown repeatedly on every station that could get their hands on it. The question of whether the officers used too much force while arresting King or if it was warranted became the hot topic conversation of the country.

After, King was taken to the hospital, where he was treated for eleven skull fractures, a broken right ankle, broken teeth, a facial bone fracture, kidney failure, and permanent brain damage, with bruises and cuts throughout his body. His blood alcohol was 0.075%, putting King over the legal limit allowed to drive and marijuana in his blood. The city decided not to charge him with driving under the influence because of his beating from officers that night.

Los Angeles Chief of Police, Daryl Gates, gave a press conference stating that he felt the officers used excessive force while arresting King. Officers had hit King between 53 to 56 times with their batons. The Los Angeles District Attorney charged the four officers with assault and the use of excessive force.

Unlike the Simpson trial we discussed earlier, they decided that having the trial in downtown Los Angeles would be unfair to the officers, so they moved the trial to Simi Valley. The jury ended up being ten white people. Even with the videotape on the seventh day of deliberation, the jury acquitted all four officers of their assault charges and excessive force charges.

After the constant airing of the King beating and arrest, and now the acquittal of all charges of the officers, the resentment that the Black community was feeling exploded. I was living, working, and going to University in Seattle at the time. It all seemed to happen so quickly after the verdict was read. Within an hour, *CNN* was showing buildings lit on fire by angry people and now burning. I headed into my job as a waiter, and when I arrived, I saw the managers outside of the restaurant boarding up the windows. What were they getting prepared for? I had grown up in Canada, where the only riots I had seen up to that date were when a city lost the Stanley Cup in the National Hockey League and nothing like what ended up happening.

A very small trickle of customers came into the restaurant, probably because everyone had their eyes glued to the news watching the riots develop in Los Angeles. It was only a matter of an hour after I got to work when I started to hear the smashing glass of different neighboring businesses and yelling outside on the streets. When I glimpsed outside from a higher window that wasn't completely covered, I saw several officers riding on horses trying to control what seemed like hundreds of people protesting the verdict.

Riots began to break out in almost every major city in the country, including San Francisco, Las Vegas, Atlanta, and New York City. These riots would last six days and cost billions of dollars in damages. It took the California National Guard, the United States Army, and the United States Marine Corps to calm things down and restore order. At the end of it all, there were 63 deaths and 2383 injuries amongst over 7000 man-made fires that damaged more than 3100 businesses.

The Rodney King beating and acquittal of the police officers who did the assault and the following city riots were still on the minds and in the hearts of most people in Los Angeles just two short years later when the murders of Nicole Brown-Simpson and Ron Goldman occurred. The unresolved and total lack of justice from that event was stuck in the pit of many stomachs. This fact is why many people in the legal profession believe the main reason Simpson was acquitted of the murder of Nicole Brown-Simpson.

Chapter 3
The Prosecution
Interview with Marcia Clark

M arcia Clark passed her bar exam in California in 1979 and worked as a public defender for Los Angeles for about two years when she became a prosecutor. By 1991, she was a deputy state attorney for the city and became famous for prosecuting Robert John Bardo for the murder of television actress Rebecca Schaeffer.

After Simpson was arrested, District Attorney Gil Garcetti chose to indict Simpson in Los Angeles instead of where the crimes occurred in Santa Monica, which meant that the trial would be held in Downtown L.A. and Marcia Clark would lead the prosecution. Her co-counsel was named Assistant District Attorney Christopher Darden.

The primary theory behind the prosecution's case was domestic abuse throughout the marriage and the jealousy of O.J. Simpson that culminated in the murder. They could easily show a history of Simpson abusing Brown throughout their marriage. Even on the night of the murders, Simpson was reportedly angry at Nicole for wearing such a tight dress at their daughter's recital.

Marcia Clark believed that Simpson drove to Nicole's condo later that evening, asking her to get back together with him. After she refused, Simpson killed her as an act of control. During this attack, Goldman dropped by her place to return the eyeglasses left at the restaurant where he worked. Goldman surprised and interrupted Simpson, who in turn attacked and killed Goldman, not wanting any witnesses.

Simpson drove home, got into his house, and changed clothing to prepare for his trip to

Chicago. He placed his bloody clothes, the knife used to murder Goldman and Brown, and the Bruno Magli shoes into his bag. He then got into the waiting limo and headed to the airport. He emptied his bag into the trash at the airport before catching his flight.

The prosecution was able to present over 100 exhibits which included 61 drops of blood they believed linked Simpson to the murders. Also presented to the jury were several hair and fiber samples that connected Simpson to the murder victims.

Verdict

All over the country, people watched the Simpson trial and listened to every commentator on television speaking to the question, "What happens if O.J. is convicted? Like in the Rodney King case, will riots break out onto the streets?" More potential riots were a genuine concern, even for law enforcement. The LAPD started running 12-hour shifts to keep the courthouse under guard. On the day the verdict came in, the LAPD sent more than 100 officers, some on horseback, to protect the courthouse and the downtown area.

On October 3, 1995, the jury came back with their verdict. At 10:07 a.m., the foreman read that Simpson was not guilty of both murder charges.

To add to the controversial trial, Lionel Cryer, Juror #9, raised his fist to salute Simpson. Apparently, Cryer was a former member of the Black Panther Party.

After the verdict was in, LAPD Police Chief Willie Williams said that they had no plans of reopening the investigation into the murders of Brown and Goldman. They also didn't reevaluate any evidence used in the trial, knowing that Simpson could not be tried again for the same case.

Interview with Marcia Clark

This Marcia Clark interview took place in 2018.

Q. You have a new book series written from the point of view of a criminal defense attorney. How did you get into writing from that point of view, as we all know you from being a prosecutor of a very popular case?

A. Right, my new series is based on Samantha Brinkman, a criminal defense lawyer with a kind of traumatic past and a very unusual view of the justice system. I started as a defense attorney in criminal law, and I shifted over to the criminal prosecution side later. Now I am handling criminal appeals for the indigent, court-appointed appeals. That's where Samantha Brinkman kind of came from. I had written a whole series on a prosecutor named Rachel Knight, and I thought I would like to stretch out and accommodate my roots and get into a more twisted character because life from the defense point of view is interesting, and it gave me an opportunity to comment on our justice system and also comment on the mentality that makes us frustrated with the way justice is sometimes administered when things can go wrong in the courtroom. And it's really fun to talk about that from the point of view of a character who is a rule breaker and really doesn't care what's legal.

Q. That brings me to a point. As a lawyer who has worked on both sides of the criminal bench like yourself, you're aware of the different roles. How do you actually describe the difference like with your new character, Samantha Brinkman's books, compared to being a prosecutor?

A. The prosecutor's job is to make sure that

a defendant is convicted but only when the evidence proves that there is evidence beyond a reasonable doubt to prove that he is guilty. And it's up to the prosecutor to make sure that the trial is fair. Do your best to make sure that you are doing it in a fair way. Not by any underhanded means, not by hiding information or twisting witness testimony, or misrepresenting things to the jury. It's your job to make sure it is done fair, cleanly, and above board.

The defense attorney has no duty to do anything except to represent the interests of his client. Now, of course, the defense is not supposed to play dirty tricks or lie to the jury, but there's kind of a slidey grey area there where they're simply presenting another point of view on the evidence and very fairly poking holes in the prosecution's case to show the jury where there's reasonable doubt. Where things were not done right, where things should have been done better, and perhaps where evidence that's helpful to the defense was overlooked. So, that's their job, to hold the prosecution's feet to the fire, which is a good thing. You want those checks and balances. No side is perfect. The prosecution, no matter how careful of the defendant's rights and the rules of court can be, sometimes they miss something. You want somebody to catch those moments. But the mindset of the defense attorney is basically, "I'm here to protect my client. I don't have to worry about the people of the State of California's right to a fair trial. I just have to take care of my client."

Q. So, I think, in essence, you're saying that the defense has a lot more creative freedom with their narrative when they're talking to the jury?

A. Well put. Yes. Very well put, and of course, as a writer, it gives you a lot more leeway to do slidey fun things, and it'll be more fun for the reader.

Q. When did you first start to get into crime in your life?

A. When I was really young. Maybe too young. This has been a lifelong fascination for me. When I was four years old, I was walking through the neighborhood looking at spots on the sidewalk, thinking that it was blood and it probably really wasn't, you know what I mean. I was a weird kid. I was always thinking in those terms of making up crime stories, even murder mysteries in my head, and reading Nancy Drew and probably books that I shouldn't be reading. As young as I was, when I was eight, I read *Compulsion*, which is the story of Leopold and Loeb, a very famous what they called a "Thrill Killing" by two very wealthy guys who just wanted to create the perfect crime, and at eight years old there's not a lot that I understood about that story. But I later reread it when it was reissued, and it's a fantastically written book.

Q. Do you miss being a prosecutor?

A. No. There was a time that I did when I first left the office. It was very weird after fourteen years of being a prosecutor. I thought I would be doing it for the rest of my life, and I had planned to. That was the whole idea. So, it took a few years for me to adjust to the idea that it was probably time to find a new life. But now that I am able to write crime fiction and practice law in a way that lets me juggle both, I kind of feel like I segued into another part of life, and I'm enjoying it.

Q. How do you feel about the justice system after being involved in it for so long and now even writing about it? Do you think it's going in the right direction; do you feel like it's a good system?

A. I feel like it has its strength and its weaknesses. My feelings about it are so ambivalent. But I just don't know a better one. Let me put it that way. I think, in general, we try to do the right thing, and in general l we try to protect the rights of both victims and defendants; in specific, not so much. There are times when the wrong thing happens. When people get convicted, that shouldn't be, and we've seen stories about that. Certainly, we've seen the stories of guilty people who don't get convicted. These things happen in a system that is run by humans. We're flawed. We make mistakes, and so it's bound to happen that mistakes will be made. There are probably ways to improve it, but I haven't seen a system that works better.

Q. How do you feel about the televising of cases?

A. This is a mixed bag for me. I usually felt that I never want cameras in the courtroom because it has an obvious impact on how cases are tried. Lawyers pander to the camera and get the nonsense motions or are just sensationalist, engaged in sensationalist rhetoric that has no place in the courtroom. Judges can pander to the limelight as well, as we saw. Witnesses come forward who maybe have nothing to say but want the limelight. Other witnesses stay away because they don't want the limelight. So, there is lots to worry about in terms of having cameras in the courtroom.

On the other hand, I think it's really important that the public knows what's going on, and I think that can have a normalizing or a balancing effect because juries can go nuts. It can happen that juries don't necessarily do the right things. I'm really not just talking about Simpson; I'm talking about in general. Weird things can happen in the courtroom, especially when a judge doesn't control the proceedings the way he should. So, it's important that the public knows about this, that they see.

I guess what I would do if I were king, what I would probably do is I would take the cameras out of the courtroom when the jury is there. If the jury can't see it, then neither should the public see it. Unless they want to come and sit in the courtroom, they're welcome to do that. I don't think there's been as much problem with print reporters reporting everything as there is with a camera, which reaches millions and millions, whereas people are less than inclined to just read about it. I think print reporters can be more accurate in terms of putting things into context. Now not necessarily as we know, print reporters can screw it up too and go for sensationalist headlines and really skew the facts to the point that they're unrecognizable. But in general, there's less danger with a print reporter sitting in the courtroom than there is with a camera. So, you ideally want to have proceedings recorded in a manner that informs the public but does not taint the jury.

Q. I just know from personal experience that when you start to perform your job in public, and you start hearing feedback about yourself, quite often, you begin to change how you act. I couldn't imagine people filming me and then people talking about what I am wearing or my hair. It would freak me out. It would change my behavior and my performance. I would come to work wearing a hat.

A. You know, why didn't I think of that?

Q. Yeah, a baseball cap!

A. (after laughing) You really have to really

make a conscious effort to disregard all of that and resist the temptation to bend with public opinion when it comes to that kind of thing. You're trying a case to a jury; you're not trying the topic to the guy across the street or the girl sitting in the park. You have to appeal to the jury that you have. Some of the people will say like, "You have to be fierier here." No, I have to appeal to this jury, not to you, to them, and the way that they perceive what's going on in court is all that matters to me and just kind of narrow focus in that way. Sometimes it's appropriate to bang the podium and scream and yell; other times, that's going to turn your jury off so much that they'll never listen to another word you say. So, you have to be in touch with who the jury is and resist the temptation to pander to people on the outside who are not the ones who matter.

Q. In Arizona, we had the Jodi Arias case, which was a really big case that was televised. When you look at Kirk Nurmi, the defense attorney for her and I have chatted and had interviews with him, and he had his life threatened. The things he had to go through because it was so public and televised. If it were me, I don't know that I could do my job properly.

A. Yes, it's scary, and I think that's so wildly inappropriate. The defense attorney has a job to do. It's an important job. We need them. We need that balance. We don't just want prosecutors up there with no answer to them. There's no question that that would lead to terrible abuses. 99 .9 percent of the prosecutors are going to do their best to be fair and impartial, but they can miss stuff. Like I said before, you need somebody sitting on the other side from the outside, poking holes in the things they don't see. If you don't have that person, then you really don't have a system of justice. It's a terrible thing, and I hate to hear that when the defense attorneys are threatened. It's unfair and a terrible thing.

Q. With televised trials such as *Making a Murderer* on Netflix, it reads the prosecutor appears to only want to get his conviction and that he was willing to do anything he could to get it. Do you think this gives a negative light on prosecutors in the country?

A. Right. That's not been my experience at all, so I can only speak from my experience.

Prosecutors, I knew nobody was out to get him no matter what. We will give up a fair trial, and then we will hang him. It's not the mentality that I ever saw. Does that mean that it doesn't exist? Of course not. There are thousands and thousands of prosecutors in this country, and there are bound to be a few bad apples. That's the way it is in every profession. There are always a few.

But in *Making of a Murderer*, that prosecutor did not come across that well. The kind of ghoulish news conferences that he was giving at the very beginning, even before he picked a jury. It's one thing to say, these are the charges, we have the evidence and that sort of thing but the gruesome details, the graphic details, not necessarily accurate details, he's already spinning the jury, and that's not appropriate. That sort of thing when you're really vilifying the defendant with yet unproven evidence is never okay to do, and I think, in hindsight, made us all say, that's too far. He shouldn't have done that. But I don't think. I hope not, anyway. I hope people don't think that's emblematic of most prosecutors.

In some respects, those documentaries can be such a good thing because they show people what's going on and what happened. But they can be a bad thing, too, if they're edited in a way that makes them inaccurate. They're leaving out important incriminating evidence, then. You don't get an accurate picture of what the case is all about and what they had against the defendant. So, I'm just hoping that these documentarians have some scruples about what they are doing so that the people are not misled.

Q. Now, both main characters found in both series of your fiction books are strong females, one a prosecutor and the other a defense attorney. How is it in the legal system in both those jobs being female? Is it equal, or what's your opinion on that?

A. So, it depends on what court you're in. The judge is the director of the show. On a film set, the director says, "cut." That's the judge. If the judge is sexist, if the judge views the female lawyer in the courtroom on either side as a second-class citizen, yep, you're going to feel it, you're going to feel it every day. You're going to feel it in the ruling. You're going to feel it in the way he behaves towards you when he talks to you in front of the jury, so it's in court that it happens.

It happened, of course, in the O.J. Simpson trial all over the place. I've never seen such condescending, demeaning behavior towards me from a judge in my entire career as a defense attorney or a prosecutor. That tells you something because the other judges, even judges who had been around in a time when there were no women in the courtroom, were much more fair, much less condescending, and demeaning than Judge Ito was. So, it depends on the courtroom.

Q. Now, the O.J. Simpson case was really huge, and there were and probably still are attorneys that have to watch that case to see how it went down. Are there, or were there any cases in history that had that kind of influence on you where you had to watch it to see how it happened, such as Charles Manson or something like that?

A. Charles Manson. That's a great example. I was pretty young when that was happening, but I remember being fascinated by why. I think that to me, in that case, that's one of those cases that the why is so mystifying. How could you, why would you, target this young woman? Senseless doesn't begin to describe it, and then your followers, who are young women, could be drawn into something like this. This horrific thing that completely befuddled me, and I was just mystified by it. I had to read *Helter Skelter* just to get a grip on it. But still, I felt like it was inexplicable. It's the kind of example of the Jonestown mentality that people can be. You get the right person at the right time, and you can convince them of almost anything, and that's terrifying.

I also remember, not long after that, being fascinated by Patricia Hearst. I can tell you that at the time of that trial, I was not yet practicing law, but shortly thereafter, not too long after that, I became a lawyer and was working at a criminal defense law firm, and it was largely the view of the criminal defense community that F. Lee Bailey screwed that case up, that it was an eminently defensible case. That she shouldn't have got acquitted but got lesser charges and that he blew it. Because there was so much evidence at the time of Stockholm Syndrome and of her being pressured and threatened and all of the things that have happened to someone who has been kept prisoner for some time.

Listen to the full interview with Marcia Clark on my website:

https://www.alanrwarren.com/
hom-podcast-episodes/
episode/e530ee38/kjll-marcia-
clark-2018-interview

Chapter 4
For the Defense
Interview with F. Lee Bailey

Meeting F. Lee Bailey was truly an interesting experience. Having grown up in the turbulent 1960s and 70s, I've heard his name on the television news regularly. He was the lawyer that appealed the Doctor Sam Sheppard case in 1966. Sheppard was accused of killing his wife in 1954, which was turned into a movie and popular television series called *The Fugitive*. Bailey also defended the "Boston Strangler" who murdered several women by strangulation.

The 1970s continued to be a busy decade for Bailey, defending the newspaper heiress Patty Hearst who was kidnapped and raped by the Symbionese Liberation Army. She was brainwashed into joining the group and going on to rob banks and kill people in the process. Bailey also defended Army Captain Ernest Medina, whose troop was responsible for what was called "The My Lai Massacre." The troop was ordered into the My Lai part of Vietnam and ordered to kill everyone there as they were all combatants. After the mass killing was over, the world found out that there were, in fact, no combatants there, just women, children, and elders. Medina was charged with 102 murders.

F. Lee Bailey had served in the military before he was a lawyer, where he started in the U.S. Navy and later the Marine Corp. After he returned from duty, he went to Harvard and then Boston University to become a lawyer in 1957.

Bailey was no stranger to being a public

lawyer taking on celebrity cases for television. He performed a fake trial on television, bringing witnesses and experts to determine if the rumor was true that Paul McCartney, one of the Beatles, was dead. Then, of course, Bailey was brought on to the "Dream Team" of lawyers to defend O.J. Simpson, and that was what we wanted our interview to be about.

On top of all that history, on February 28, 1982, Bailey was pulled over and arrested for being intoxicated while driving a motor vehicle. Bailey's arrest upset him so much that he ended up writing a book about his experience and how to protect yourself against cops in California, which not only explained how to defend yourself when being pulled over but also told of the alleged abuses the police were responsible for.

In 2001, Bailey was disbarred in Florida because while he was defending marijuana dealer Claude DuBoc, he transferred most of DuBoc's assets and his shares in the pharmaceutical company Biochem Pharma into his own bank account. The issue was that DuBoc had agreed to a plea bargain where he would forfeit his stocks in Biochem Pharma which was worth about 6 million dollars. When law enforcement found out that Bailey had these stocks, they ordered him to surrender them to the government. He refused. Bailey claimed that the stocks were payment for his work in defending DuBoc. During the time period of this legal battle, those stocks rose to about $20 million in value, so Bailey agreed that the government could sell off the stocks if he could keep the difference in value. Bailey was imprisoned for contempt of court for not surrendering the stocks to the court, where he ended up serving six weeks. He was released after finally turning the stock over. He was found guilty of seven counts of attorney misconduct and disbarred. After years of failed legal battles to get his license to practice law back, he decided to start a consulting business in Maine.

On the morning of the day we were to interview Bailey, my cell phone rang. When I answered it and said "hello," there was a long silence. "Hello?" Again, another long silence. I was about to hang up when I suddenly heard a deep stern voice say, "You are going to interview me today?" This time I was silent, as I wasn't sure who this was and how they got my cell phone number. I thought quickly that we were interviewing F. Lee Bailey. Could this be him?

"You are the man interviewing me today?' the

man said again, this time a little louder and even more stern, maybe even angry sounding.

"Oh, is this Mr. Bailey?"

"Yes."

"Oh, okay. Yes, we are interviewing you today. Was there something you needed?"

"No. Do you see a phone number on your phone?"

"Yes."

"That's my cell number. Call me back when you are ready."

I started to respond by saying something like, "Yes, sir, I will," only he hung up as soon as he finished speaking.

I turned to look at my cohost and stared at him before he said, "What was that?"

"That was F. Lee Bailey, and I don't know what that was?"

"Well, what did he want?"

"He just wanted me to know that this was his cell number. But we're calling him on his landline. So, why does he want me to call him on his cell phone when we're ready? This is going to be a hard one!"

Bailey passed away one week before his 88 birthday on June 3, 2021, in Atlanta, Georgia.

Defense Case

The so-called defense "Dream Team" for the O.J. Simpson case was built by Simpson's first lawyer for this case, Robert Shapiro. He brought on F. Lee Bailey, Robert Kardashian, Alan Dershowitz, and The Innocence Project's Barry Scheck. At first, they were running a standard defense of reasonable doubt until Simpson hired lawyer Johnnie Cochrane.

Cochrane took it in a whole new direction by attacking the evidence and the detectives who gathered the evidence. He also attached it to race, which relit the anger from the Rodney King case two years earlier. Mark Fuhrman, the detective who found the blood evidence and glove, was shown to be a racist. After the Fuhrman tapes were released, showing his hate for black people, it was easy to pursue.

If the glove doesn't fit, you must acquit!

One of the key pieces of evidence, in this case, was the glove that was found at the Simpson property. A few months before the trial even began, there were published articles claiming that the defense was going to be able to prove that detective Mark Fuhrman planted the glove with blood on it on O.J.'s property because he hated black people.

F. Lee Bailey had made the statement that Fuhrman found the glove at the crime scene at Nicole Brown-Simpson's residence, picked it up with a stick, put it in a plastic bag, and hid it from the other detectives when he arrived at Simpson's house. Then, as soon as he found a chance, he dropped the glove to frame Simpson.

Marcia Clark denied the claim that Fuhrman planted the glove and that he was racist toward black people. She also had Lt. Frank Spangler testify that he was with Fuhrman the whole time that they were searching Simpson's property. Not only was Fuhrman never alone, but Spangler would have seen it if Fuhrman had planted the glove. Spangler also brought up the fact that when they arrived at Simpson's residence, they didn't know any of the details of the murder case. He wouldn't have known who was considered a suspect at the time, whose blood was on the glove, or if there were any witnesses to the murders. It all seemed to be going well for the prosecution until Fuhrman was cross-examined by the defense.

Bailey asked Fuhrman if he had ever used the

word "nigger" to describe African Americans in the previous ten years. Fuhrman denied ever using that word at work or home. A few months after that testimony by Fuhrman, audiotapes happened to be discovered and given to the defense team. These tapes would later be labeled as the "Fuhrman Tapes." On these tapes, Fuhrman could be heard saying the word "nigger" a total of 41 times.

After the tapes were released, Fuhrman asked for Clark to bring him back up onto the stand so that he could help explain why he used the word and put it into context so that the jury would understand it. But the prosecution and a lot of other detectives stayed clear from Fuhrman as they didn't want to be associated with him or what he said on the tapes. The defense brought him back to the stand to ask more questions since the prosecution wouldn't. This time Fuhrman's personal lawyer told him to plead the fifth on all questions so as not to incriminate himself.

In June, Darden, co-counsel and Assistant District Attorney, surprised Marcia Clark and much of the courtroom by asking Simpson to try on the glove that was found at the Brown's residence. Clark had made the decision not to ask Simpson to try on the glove as it had been through several lab tests, including being frozen a few times, not to mention it was soaked in blood, so it would be too risky. In fact, Clark had already brought witnesses to testify that Simpson had bought the gloves from Bloomingdales in 1990 and also supplied the receipt and pictures of Simpson wearing those gloves. So, when Simpson stood up in front of the whole courtroom while being televised for everyone to see, the gloves were too tight for him to fit on his hand.

After the trial was over, Cochrane revealed that it was Bailey who egged on Darden to ask for Simpson to try on the bloody glove in court.

Police Conspiracy to Frame O.J. Simpson

The defense team created a whole narrative that there was a police conspiracy against O.J. Simpson, and they were all involved in the planting of evidence. This would be the only way to eliminate forensic or blood evidence that tied the murders to Simpson as being valid. They would detail every step that detectives made in gathering evidence from the crime scene. Barry Scheck brought up the fact that while police were handling evidence, they never once changed their gloves between items. This could mean cross-contamination between items. Police also used plastic bags, and they were supposed to use paper bags. Detectives also ended up storing evidence in a police van for over seven hours without refrigeration which could degrade the DNA on items.

But the defense team's key piece of evidence to not only prove that Simpson didn't commit the murders and that the police were planting evidence and trying to frame him was the EDTA. Ethylenediaminetetraacetic (EDTA) is a preservative used by authorities in order to keep blood samples over a period of time so that they can test and retest the samples several times. It is kept in the vials where samples are stored.

Human blood also has a certain level of EDTA in it naturally, but not near the levels that are found in police stored samples. So, after the blood samples found at the crime scene were tested for EDTA and found to be higher than normal, it was the defense's theory that detective Fuhrman actually went to the police station where police had taken a sample of O.J.'s blood for testing, and taken it to the crime scene and planted it.

Cochrane had an expert witness, Dr. Rieder, testify that the level of EDTA that he discovered in the blood samples was too high to have occurred naturally. Therefore, the blood was taken from stored police vials and placed at the scene, and it wasn't there from the murders. Later, it was determined that the EDTA tests that Rieder did were inconclusive and, in fact, he had read the numbers wrong. But by this time, the damage had been done, and the jury was already suspicious of the evidence that the prosecutors had presented.

The blood collected from the crime scene on Brown's back gate was the next sample brought into question by the defense. They told the jury that the blood was not collected on June 13, which was the day following the murders, because it wasn't there. Scheck displayed an enlarged picture of the gate that was taken by police on that date and showed that there was no blood on the gate then. He went on to say that it was collected on July 3rd after it had been planted there.

Again, the prosecution tried to counter this theory by bringing up officer Robert Riske, who was the first officer at the scene and also the one to point out the blood on the gate to detective Fuhrman, and he had his notes with him in court to prove this. The prosecution then presented their own enlarged photograph of the fence from June 13th and was able to show the jury the blood on the gate.

Next, the defense brought into question the bloody socks that were found in O.J.'s bedroom the day after the murders. These socks ended up having both O.J.'s and Nicole's blood on them. These socks were also found by detective Fuhrman whom they had already brought up for planting the glove evidence. The defense claimed that detective Vannatter was the one who planted the bloody socks and told Fuhrman where they were so that he could find them. Vannatter received blood samples of both Nicole and O.J. earlier that day, and this gave him the opportunity to place the blood on Simpson's socks earlier that day.

Even though the prosecution was able to show a film of Vannatter when he arrived at the crime scene as well as prove the socks had already been discovered and bagged before he got there, again, the damage was done.

Interview with F. Lee Bailey

This interview took place with lawyer F. Lee Bailey in the summer of 2017.

After the pre-interview phone call that Bailey gave me, I was a little worried. After we connected with Bailey on his landline located in his office, he remained stern and to the point. So, the interview started out very formal and uptight until he discovered I was far more interested in some of his less well-known cases. When we told him that we thought his best cases were the Medina and Hearst case, he loosened right up and even started to crack some jokes. You never know what questions will loosen up a guest like Bailey!

Q. You've done many cases. Out of all the points you've done, is there one that stays with you now? It's not necessarily the most popular case, of course, but is there a case that you think about a lot?

A. The two cases I think you are looking for are of very different types. In both cases, they involve murder. One is Doctor Sam Sheppard, who became the TV show *The Fugitive*, who became the movie *The Fugitive*, and whom I got out of the life sentence and defended on retrial, and was acquitted tragically after he died. Probably OD.

DNA evidence came forward, although belated, showing that there was someone else in the house that night where the murder occurred. Oddly enough, the prosecution then stipulated that if there were any proof that someone else was there, they wouldn't charge Doctor Sheppard. So, essentially, they put the burden on the defense before there was even an indictment.

It's still one of the most perplexing and widely known in the history of American murder cases. But more than that, it set the standard for balancing the press and the right to a fair trial. It's still being navigated and fleshed out, and I've been a part of it most of the way since I argued that case. I've had the privilege of having Justice Tom Clark say to me, "Did you like my opinion in the Sheppard case?" and I said, "Your honor, I thought it was wonderful." Which is a way of saying, "Yes, we won." He said, "You should. I took it right out of your brief." I will tell you, that is flattering.

Q. One of the things that made this case so famous was that he was denied Due Process. Would you explain a little bit about that to the listeners?

A. Well, I think the best source one should go to is because one shouldn't always take a lawyer's enthusiasm as gospel when he's talking about a crime, particularly in a case that he has won. But if one is to look back in history, the 1964 opinion in the U.S. District Court in the Southern District of Ohio written by Chief Judge Carl Weinman, said this, "I found five constitutional flaws in the Sheppard conviction, each of which would warrant a new trial on its own." That opinion was upheld by the U.S. Supreme Court.

Q. We have also had guests on before that have talked about Dorothy Kilgallen being involved in the Sam Sheppard trial. Can you tell us about that?

A. Yes, I can because it was fascinating. She was there right at the very beginning. Dorothy Kilgallen, apart from her place on one of the game shows, was a very bright woman, and her father, Jim Kilgallen, was a well-known and respected crime reporter in the New York area. Dorothy, in the capacity of a reporter, went to see the trial judge in the first trial in 1954, whose name was Edward Blythin, and he was very excited that a reporter of her national import would show up in his humble little court in Cuyahoga County in Ohio, and he invited her into his chamber, and he was very cordial. He was then running for re-election.

He said, "Miss Kilgallen, why have you come to little old Cleveland here to cover this case? You're a woman of great national importance." She said, "Judge, I think you got a real who-done-it here, and a real who-done-it. America's fascinated." Blythin said, "Well, no who-done-it. It's clear that Sheppard did it." Then he proceeded to sit on the bench as a neutral judge. This evidence was new and had never been studied before. I found out about it by attending a talk in New York where it was mentioned, so I went to see her, and she told me all the details. So, we took her deposition, and that was filed before a federal judge. So, the Supreme Court turned the case on the judge, saying that it was up to the judge to balance the interest of a fair trial and the free press should trump but, the press is not to be squelched, and that is the rule of law pretty much today in the United States of America. Frankly, by different bits of language, I think in most Anglo-American countries.

Q. I have to ask what your thoughts are surrounding Dorothy's death as there are a lot of writers who have claimed she was murdered and did not die of an overdose.

A. I spent not a night but an evening with Dorothy Kilgallen because after Sam Sheppard was released, she came to town to interview him, and I invited him to have a couple of drinks in my hotel because I was very grateful that she had stood up after all of those years and correctly recited what the judge had said, which ordinarily as a reporter, as you guys know, would never do. You don't identify sources for anything, but the greater injustice was that Sam Sheppard was in jail. She had watched the trial and was satisfied that he should have been back fitted, and so she came forward.

I spent two or three hours with her drinking, you know, more than one cocktail, and as the evening we on, I could see that Dorothy was despondent and in a terrible state of mind. But I did not do anything heroic to help her. I was concerned about her, and the next thing I heard two days later was she had killed herself. I have no reason to think that she was murdered then, and I think at least the underground would have put out a current of information if somebody had knocked her off because that's a level of information that the press seldom gets a look in on.

Q. Would you mind talking about the Ernest Medina case and your involvement in that case?

A. It shows the length and depth of your research because if you had asked me, "Okay, you told us about the Sheppard case, what would the second one be?" It was Captain Ernest Medina. The whole of Vietnam was terribly distasteful, and this was the bottom point of all the ugliness of the Vietnam War. A Captain named Medina, who was a commander and had several platoons under him, one of which was headed by a Lieutenant named Calley, and they were told in defense of everybody in the village of Ma Lai, you're going to encounter combatants, and you should go in shooting and take them out and then kill all of the livestock so that families won't come back to the village. The soldiers had moved on the intelligence, which was bad, and Medina was not there. He arrived after it happened.

But Calley and his platoon went into Ma Lai and found no combatants. They found women holding infants in their arms, children by their hands, older adults, and other minors not yet adults, and in Vietnam in those days, if you were eleven or twelve, they'd put you in uniform. Calley and his crew shot all of those people. Those babies, those women, and so forth. Then the army had covered it up, at least those who knew about it. Medina covered it up too, but he never got charged with that. Calley got convicted, and Medina was charged with killing 102 people, 10 of whom were unnamed.

The thing I liked about the case because it is on its face, and certainly as it emerged in *Time Magazine* in 1969 with bloody photographs from an army photographer who was on the scene and recorded the event. It was absolutely filthy, and I think opposite to everything this country believes in, or at least says that it does.

On the other side, this was a tough case with conflicts all over the place. The army wanted liability cut off at a junior level. In other words, Calley was guilty. Medina was guilty. His commanding officer was guilty, nobody else. So, Calley, Medina, and Colonel Henderson were tried. But Medina came to me, and I agreed to defend him for $3000 bucks, which he put up. I had a couple of superb lawyers, one of whom was Harry Truman's grandnephew. They were assigned to me to assist in defending Medina, and they were wonderful. I hired both of them the minute I could get them out of uniform. The prosecutor was a tough guy but a fair guy.

Q. You were a Marine?

A. I was a Marine, and I understood the military mindset. The military mindset is to make sure you don't convict an innocent person. If you condemn innocent people in the military, even a couple, you won't get reenlisted, so don't let it happen. That was our concentration. I wish it were the rule of law in the civilian sector because there are so many politics that infuse, and I think it infests the civilian sector in both state and federal justice systems that we find things like 95 guys on death row who turned out to be innocent. My lord, how dysfunctional is a system that could do that?

Q. Now, if I remember this right, the only thing Medina could be connected to was a woman in a ditch that he thought had explosives on her. Did he shoot her? Did his men shoot her?

A. You're close. The woman was not in a ditch. That's down. She was on a ledge, that's up. She was pretending to be dead. Medina walked up to her, and as he turned away, he saw her move. And according to the evidence in the trial, several witnesses said, "Oh my God, a grenade!" He whirled and shot at her. Another witness, I think it was Staff Sergeant, said, "I saw it all happen." He has told the truth, except he said, "He missed, and I shot her, and we both thought that she was going to shoot us." That's one of the 102 murders that didn't make a whole lot of sense as far as Medina is concerned.

Q. Another case that I noticed that you were a part of was the "Boston Strangler," Albert DeSalvo.

A. Yes.

Q. Now, did he actually confess his guilt to being the "Boston Strangler" to you?

A. Well, it happened this way, and it's much more convoluted than that, but I can boil it down for you rather quickly. I had a client who was on indictment for murder and was in an institution in Mass. [Massachusetts] He asked me to come to talk to a guy and said, "I think he might be the Strangler." Well, I said, "Next time

I see you, I'll give him a few minutes, I'm. I'm really interested in that."

I did talk with Albert DeSalvo, and he made it pretty plain that he would like to write a book about strangling women if his family, not he, his family, could get some income from it because he had pretty much made out that he was not going to be free again. So, I followed up on that with some onside detectives. Figured out some questions that only the guilty party in each case would know. Albert answered all of them correctly, or at least very substantially correctly, and the investigation ceased, and the focus was on Albert. The deal I made for him was, you could talk to him [Albert] all you want only on the guardianship, which means he's incompetent to wave his fifth amendment rights, which means you can use anything you can get to use on your book, but you cannot use it against Albert DeSalvo. I got that agreement, and I got his guardian to be appointed, and he gave 65 hours of details about the strangling describing the homicides he committed, which we call twelve and a half because one of the victims was 88, and we think she died of a heart attack although there was evidence of a ligature around her neck, she just didn't live long enough to become strangled. But he gave 65 hours of description to the homicide chief of the Mass. State Police, the homicide chief of Boston, the assistant attorney general, and the guardian who was the former commissioner of corrections and lawyer.

Q. I also wanted to ask you about Patty Hearst and her comments about you having a disjointed closing statement. What is your memory of Patty Hearst?

A. Well, my memory of Patty Hearst is that her evaluation of her trial is very inaccurate and, I think, not forthcoming. I've always believed in Patty Hearst, and I still do. I don't think she should have been convicted because she was truly brainwashed. But Patty doesn't start in the right place, maybe because she wasn't there. The two people who we are no longer with us.

Randy Hearst called me, got right through the red tape to the Warden, and then to me when I was in prison with an inmate in Jackson, Mississippi, and he said, "I need you to come here as fast as you can." So, I hopped in my airplane, flew to San Francisco, and got there at one in the morning. He said, "I know you've read all about his, and Patty is in much trouble robbing banks and blowing up the police station, but there's only one case that bothers. It's first-.It's murder. If she gets convicted, their or your name could be ruined. She may never get out of prison, and I want you to handle that case and anything you can along the way."

That's exactly what we did. She admits in her book that she got away with murder in the first degree. She does not say thank you for getting me out of that, but we negotiated with the FBI and the Justice Department, and she was never charged. Although others were and have pleaded to that crime. Others who were in on the robbery where two people got murdered. As far as her case was concerned, I thought the judge did a terrible thing when he assured Patty and me that the bank robbery with the murder would never get brought to her bank robbery case in San Francisco. You know there was Sacramento, which was the Hibernia Bank, and after I put her on the stand because she was just about dead from lack of blood to the brain, and as it turned out a few weeks later, he changed his mind and decided to let them ask about the Sacramento case, and there we stood. So, 42 times she took the fifth, the most times I had seen that happen in a Federal Court. I don't think she should have been convicted, but it is the worst case I have ever had in my career.

Q. Do you think she was involved with the Liberation Army?

A. There's no question that she was never involved with them until she got kidnapped. There's no question. But once she got kidnapped, after that, we have her story without very much contradiction, and that was that she was kept in the closet and that she was allowed by a supervisor to go to the bathroom from time to time. At the head of the self-styled SLA, Donald DeFreeze, or Cinque as he liked to be known, I think there's no question that he had sex with her, and I would have to call it rape when you lock someone in a closet on many occasions. But ultimately, I think it's very clear that Patty Hearst was brainwashed into thinking the following because it's really a Stockholm Syndrome case which is a pretty well-known psychosomatic problem. That is when you are convinced that your captives are your only chance if you step outside the cocoon, that machine gun will be resigning from all the bad guys, and that includes all the cops and former friends and so forth. So, you better hang out with this group. It's your only salvation.

We've had pilots go through that all the time. They made confessions to germ warfare, nuclear warfare, and all kinds of bad things during their career, and we find that there's no way to stop that process from being. If Patty Hearst had been black or poor, she probably would have never been charged. If she had been black and poor, she would have been out the door.

Q. In her memoirs, what she had written about the trial, she had some problems with your approaches. How about you describe what it was like to represent her and some of the problems she had with your representation?

A. Well, Patty Hearst, at best, is a quarterback with 20-20 hindsight. Once she took the fifth amendment, there was no way that her case on that bank robbery could have gone any other way. On the one hand, I don't think that she was a criminal. On the other hand, she should thank her lucky stars that she is not now in jail without ever having any afterlife because whoever drives a getaway car in a bank robbery where murder is committed is liable for the murder. She was liable for the murder of the pregnant woman who got gunned down in the bank robbery by the woman who kidnapped Patty Hearst.

Patty, at the time of the trial, did what she was told. She never had the basis for critiquing the trial, but I am sure her publisher had said, as many have said to me, you've got to spice this up a bit, and if you attack F. Lee Bailey, it always gets news when you attack your defense lawyer, it always gets numbers. Because Patty Hearst never said a word to me about any criticisms or shortcomings. If that had been her view, we would not have been kept on as her lawyers who appealed the case, and we were.

Q. There were rumors that were floating around, and she alluded to these in her writing about alcohol abuse, but you considered representing her even in the face of these rumors. Did that affect your judgment at all?

A. The rumors were never there. I was picked up in 1983, long after the Hearst case had gone to bed, and we were no longer in litigation except in the executive clemency hearings. Carter had given her a commendation, and eventually, Clinton pardoned her. If Carter had been pardoned, the DA in Sacramento was going to indict her for murder, and she would have had no defense because although her statement to the FBI saying that she was there could not be used against her, she wrote a book saying I did it. Books are admissible evidence.

People thought that it was too late and nobody was going to bother. But all that aside, quite not relevant to the Hearst case, except I think in the mind of the cop who arrested me, I was going through a stop sign in San Francisco in 1982, I believe. I was tried before a jury in 1983, and the issue was that I had too much to drink. They tried to bring in witnesses, and they did. Unfortunately for them, the witnesses said, "Mr. Bailey never drinks too much, and we felt that he did that night," and the jury came back with a verdict in a snap.

So, Patty's suspicion has never been fleshed out at all. Nor did she have the suspicion. Somebody said that to her long after the trial was over. I put no stock in it, and I doubt that if we were to have the ability to take her deposition today, she would not be able to cite a single source except rumors which are not admissible in any court in the world.

Q. Now, we should talk about the O.J. Simpson case.

A. Yes.

Q. What is your impression of how it was handled by the prosecution?

A. The O.J. Simpson case is a blight upon the history of the United States, and I can sum it up in no other way. It was a case that should not have been brought and would not have been if it were not for the fact that the LAPD was smarting from the consequences of the Rodney King case. They made several quantum leaps for lack of evidence and what Johnny Cochrane called a rush to judgment. It was lousy police work. The prosecutors assigned should never have been involved in the murder case. If there had been a case against O.J., they would not have been unable to make it out.

But I must tell you that if I had been hired by L.A. to prosecute O.J., with much experience and a lot of pretty good skills, I could not have made out a case against O.J. because he wasn't there. He had a timeline bar, also known as a component alibi, and that means that although no one could say that they were with me when the murder happened, I could prove that twenty minutes before then, I was with Al Warren. Ten minutes before that, I was with Lee Bailey, and twelve minutes after it happened, I was with Bill Belichick. Twenty minutes after it happened, I was with Tom Brady.

So, unless you believe at least one and probably more of these people, I could not have committed the crime. We had that kind of evidence of O.J. The jury decided on it very quickly. We think the amount of time they deliberated was probably less than an hour. We know they signed the verdict form within three hours of me having gotten the case, and yet never in my life have I seen the turn on somebody acquitted by the jury and say that the jury was racist, that they were stupid, and that the case is a mess. Before I die, which isn't going to happen for a while, I will straighten out the O.J. Simpson case. It ain't happened yet in twenty-four years.

Q. How do you plan on doing that?

A. Several ways. First of all, there was a good reaction by the public to O.J.'s testimony at the parole hearing. He would not testify in either the L.A. or Las Vegas trials. The public didn't get a look at him. He's a very good witness, I think. If O.J. Simpson kills anybody, it'll be by telling them to death. A violent man with weapons, he is not. I have introduced him to many people. He's a nice man. But he made a good impression on the public during the parole hearing, and he's being released in October. CBS is planning to re-air a special on this California case on September 30th. NBC has done a special focusing on the robbery case in Las Vegas, and I'm told it will air late this year.

Q. They have pictures of O.J. getting onto a plane with a gym bag. Now in the very beginning of the O.J. case, they made a big deal about what was in this gym bag and why are they letting him leave with a gym bag.

A. You know why? My memory is not flawless, but it's as close as you're likely to see. When it comes to the O.J. case, I can pull almost any details, but for the ones that I cannot pull up, McKenna, my chief investigator, can. The answer to your question is that they wondered about the gym bag, and they asked that it be opened. Robert Kardashian, who lent O.J. his home at the time, opened that bag and photographed its contents with nothing in it. So that supposed piece of evidence with bloody clothes and crap like that which was preposterous, I mean, the gym bag was coming back from Chicago. He got on the plane going to Chicago with me, and who would take bloody clothes to Chicago and then bring them back so that the cops might catch him?

It was one of the very many, and this is tragic, I think, the very many silly points of the O.J. Simpson trial. It was much more circus than trial. It was a trial of many mistakes and much wasted time, but it was solved by only one issue at the end of the day, how did the glove that had once been on the hand of the killer get to O.J.'s house? It seems like there are only two answers. Did O.J. plant it there, or did Fuhrman drop it there to keep himself in a case? Where he had just been relieved of duty in favor of more senior detectives, and the answer is very simple. You'll find it on my website *BaileyandElliot.com*, which not only contains the Fuhrman tapes, where he, I think, on 42 occasions, one describes black people in an unflattering way. But you'll also find an experiment we conducted that proved that O.J. couldn't have dropped the glove. That issue is going to be fleshed out much better in the book I'm working on, hopefully.

Q. How do you explain markings that were on O.J.'s hand that were consistent with a stabbing?

A. The answer to that is that he did not. There were no defensive wounds. One of the few good things Ron Shapiro did in the case early on was to bring on Doctor Robert Huizenga, who is a very good man, a very good doctor, and who conducted the experiment that showed that O.J. could not have planted the glove. Huizenga inspected O.J. from top to bottom to see if he had any wounds, lesions, or abrasions that might be consistent with having been involved in a fight where the victim got stabbed with a knife seventeen times, which being Ron Goldman.

In Nicole's case, she wasn't stabbed that many times but they all but cut her head off. They severed the neck from the head. There I had the doctor examine O.J. to show where he was not hurt. There was a cut on his finger. That is so well accounted for with a broken glass with his blood on it in the bathroom in the hotel in Chicago where he had planned to stay. He wrapped some towel around t, went down to the front desk, and said, "I've got to go back to L.A. I won't be at the golf tournament.

Could you give me a band-aid?" They did, and that is the only wound on his body, obviously made by that broken glass because he was holding it when he got the call from detective Ron Phillips, "Nicole has been murdered." He crushed the glass and broke it.

Q. The tapes. Did it make a difference in the case?

A. I think we won the case easily without the tapes where the public was concerned. I think it showed Fuhrman was both a racist and a liar, and I think they were very valuable. Unfortunately, and this is what people don't know, we got cut off about twenty percent of the way through this investigation for one reason. We had fourteen working jurors left. One was 73, one was complaining about angina pains, and that brought us to twelve. The ability to move forward and finish the case would depend on the prosecution saying we would agree to go forward with less than twelve. Marcia Clark told the judge, "No way. We want the mistrial." People that think they have a good case don't ask for a mistrial, usually.

Q. Well, who did it then, or did you find a suspect?

A. Well, again, if someone sits off the radar, the FBI made some inquiries, and their best info was that Faye Resnick, who was living with Nicole until the day before the murder, owed substantial funds for the purchase of cocaine and she was institutionalized the day before the murder. Some hitman trying to collect the money for cocaine, thought to be about 30 grand, came to get it and thought Nicole was Faye. And when Nicole gave them a very hard time, as I'm very sure she did, she got her throat cut. As she was dying, Ron Goldman came down from the restaurant less than a block away to return some eyeglasses that Nicole's mother had left when Nicole and her mother had eaten there an hour before. That's the best we can piece it together. Because the LAPD spent so much time prosecuting O.J., if the killer came forward today and said I can prove that I did it with pictures of me cutting her throat, they would probably kill the killer and the photographer.

Listen to the full interview with F. Lee Bailey on my website:

https://www.alanrwarren.com/hom-
podcast-
episodes/episode/b3fb4319/f-lee-
bailey-O.J.-simpson-trial-lawyer

Chapter 5
The Survivors
Interview with Kim Goldman

Ron Goldman was friends with Nicole Brown-Simpson, and she was a regular customer in the restaurant where he worked.

Early that June night, Nicole ate there with her mother and some other friends. After the Browns finished their dinner and left, the manager realized that one of them had left a pair of glasses at the table, so he called Nicole at her home. Ron, a waiter there, overheard the manager calling Nicole and volunteered to drop off the glasses after he finished up at work, which would only be another ten or twenty minutes.

Later that fateful night, Ron walked the glasses over to Nicole's place as he knew where she lived, and it was only a couple of minutes away. Having worked as a waiter in my twenties, I remember how many of my customers I got to know and even ended up socializing with them and becoming friends. So, that is not unusual for people who believe this scenario isn't true.

Kim Goldman became a regular face we saw over the Simpson trial period. Daily, she sat in court with her father, looking for justice for the murder of her brother, Ron, while arranging his funeral and burial. All while dealing with the grief of his brutal murder and being suddenly thrown into the spotlight of everybody in the world.

Two years after the murders, Fred Goldman and Sharon Rufo, Ron Goldman's parents, and Lou Brown, Nicole Brown-Simpson's father, filed a joint civil lawsuit against O.J. Simpson. Many differences existed between the original trial and this one.

First, unlike in the first trial, the judge, in this case, wouldn't allow cameras in the court. The judge also wouldn't let Simpson's defense attorney, Robert Baker, use racism by the Los Angeles Police Department or any of their members, and he wouldn't allow him to put down the crime lab that worked the case.

Overall, the physical evidence remained the same, but there was additional testimony by witnesses and experts about domestic violence in the home. A couple of essential pieces of evidence were presented in this trial. The Goldman's attorney, Daniel Petrocelli, showed a picture of O.J. Simpson, predating the murders, where he was wearing Bruno Magli shoes. In the first trial, he claimed he never owned a pair. Petrocelli also brought forward a lie detector test that detectives gave Simpson during the original investigation, which showed he was deceptive when asked if he committed the murders of Goldman and Nicole. Simpson had denied ever having been given a polygraph test, which turned out to be another lie.

Another critical difference in this trial

compared to the first was that O.J. Simpson testified on his own behalf this time. But Petrocelli caught him in several lies while he was testifying. Officer Mark Fuhrman did not testify in this trial.

At the end of the civil trial, the jury found Simpson responsible for the deaths of both Nicole Brown-Simpson and Ron Goldman. It awarded the victim's families $33.5 million in compensation and punitive damages. Simpson almost immediately filed for bankruptcy and moved to Florida since, in that state, his pension could not be seized or garnished. Simpson's remaining assets were taken by authorities and auctioned off to help pay off some of the awards to the families. Goldman says that to date, they have only received about 1 percent of the $33.5 million awarded, or $335,000.

If I Did It by O.J. Simpson

A very controversial thing to happen around this case was in November of 2006, O.J. Simpson published a book called *If I Did It* through Regan Books. They released it at the same time as a Fox Special that featured Simpson aired. But mass criticism over the whole project was enough to make Fox cancel their television special. The book was released but later was given to the Goldman family to manage with hopes of paying off some of the judgment they were awarded from Simpson in court.

Kim has moved on since then, writing books, doing podcasts, and helping victims of awful crimes. During this interview, Kim was no longer saying O.J. Simpson's name. Throughout this interview, she refers to him as "The Killer." We were interested to learn her thoughts about the justice system, the civil trial, the media during such things, and all the players involved in the trial.

Interview with Kim Goldman

This interview took place in 2019.

Q. It's been 25 years since the trial for the murder of your brother Ron Goldman took place. How do you look back on that now, and how was your brother represented during that trial?

A. I guess I would say that I try to separate that a little bit because I don't think that the overall trial was a representation of my brother because he was not very well acknowledged. In that case, he was always referred to as the friend or the other victim. But I think that what trial and the subsequent information we learned after the fact, the civil case, etc., really demonstrates the injustice in our country. You know, we talk about race and celebrityism and how things went wrong in that case, and I also get to talk about my brother being a hero, so I think those two things are separate.

Q. When we go back in time, how old were you, and what was going on in your life when the murders happened?

A. I was 22 and a half, probably. I was living in San Francisco, finishing up my schooling, and I was working full-time at Wells Fargo Bank and doing an internship at a psychiatric hospital, and applying for grad school.

Q. What did you want to graduate in?

A. Psychology. I was one of those weird kids that knew exactly what she wanted to be at six. I always wanted to be a child psychologist, and I benefitted so much from therapy growing up that I wanted to be able to do that for a career.

Q. So, how did this murder impact that? Were you able to complete your degree, or did you ever go back into that field, or did you change totally?

A. I did not finish, and I did not continue down that path at the time. I focused my attention on my brother and what was needed in Los Angeles at the time. I ended up in a couple of weird jobs after that and then found my way back into the nonprofit life. So I worked with a handful of organizations that work with people with autism. Now I'm running an organization called the "Youth Project," which provides free mental health to teenagers, and I've been here since 2005. So, I did make my way back years later. I get to work with kids now and help them deal with suicide, depression, and grief.

Q. You've been out talking in public and doing your podcast, but one of the comments that Oprah Winfrey asked aimed at you was, "Why don't you move on?" How do you respond to that?

A. The same way I did all those years ago when she said that to me, which is, "How do you expect me to do that?" We don't have complete control over what the media does, we don't have full control over what the killer does, and because he still commands so much attention, I'm left on the receiving end of that, and so even if, in theory, or in my fantasy world I wanted to have a killer-free existence in my life, I don't get to do that because he is who he is and I just have to figure out ways to compartmentalize it, figure out a way not to let it suffocate me and that takes much energy. Some days I choose to engage with it, and sometimes I don't. It doesn't mean that it's not out there. But it's a part of me, and it's attached to me, so I just have to figure out a way to deal with it.

Q. Yes, but I think that it's offensive to say such a thing, and who is Oprah to say such a thing? Has she gone through this kind of trauma?

A. But I think the term "move on" insinuates that you put something behind you, that you've gotten over it. That's what that phrase sort of means for me. I move forward. Sometimes I move left, and sometimes I go backward, and sometimes I go right. That's kind of how grief works, it's not linear, and I'm trying to honor my grief and my loss and what we've experienced as a family, and it's going to look different for me than it does for other people. I wish that was more respected than judged.

Q. How does that work for you now? How do you choose and trust people that you meet and date? How do you analyze that?

A. I don't. I don't do a very good job. That's why I am still single. You know it's hard. My therapists are surprised at how trusting I am after all that I have experienced in my life. I think as I have gotten a little bit older, my guard has gone up a little bit more than when I was younger, partly because I just don't have the energy to deal with other people's b.s. sometimes. I do have a fear of being taken advantage of, you know, not being seen for who I am. I think I see things differently than I did when I was younger, but I'm trying. It's a work in progress, as I hope I always am for the rest of my life.

Q. Now, you have taken ownership of the book written by O.J. Simpson, *If I Did It*, as well as having made some changes to the book. Was that part of the lawsuit, and is that why you were doing that?

A. Yes. We were ordered to take ownership of the book. It's a little nuance, but I think it's important. We didn't want the book published when we first heard about it, and we didn't want him to benefit from it, which he did. So, when that happened, because there was still a judgment, our attorneys put a lien on the book and on the company that owned the book. It was a shell company he created to funnel funds through, so that book put the company into bankruptcy. The only asset of that company was the book. The judge ordered us to monetize the book in order to pay off the bankruptcy, fees and debt that he owed. It's a little tricky there, but once we acquired rights to the book, we were ordered to publish it. So we did. We sort of had to embrace it and rewrite it as a confession at that time.

Q. You've never really received any part of, or very little of, the 33 million dollars that you were awarded, correct?

A. Yes, the 33 and a half million that I was awarded between the estate for Nicole Brown and my dad or our family. That amount has grown over time because there's the interest added every year. But I think our portion to date is like in the 80 million range. But no, we've been unsuccessful in our pursuits. He's very much insulated by the law and by what he is required to pay. He's very much protected, and the civil system doesn't afford any resources for people trying to collect from their judgment.

Q. When you look back at the trial, where do you think it went wrong, and do you blame anyone for it?

A. I place blame on the killer first and foremost. But I think that Judge Ito lost control of the courtroom, and I think that in doing so created a chaotic atmosphere, and so everything was up for grabs. And I think the jury fell for that hook, line, and sinker. No matter what the prosecution did or what evidence they had, I don't think that they were willing to see it, and I don't know exactly why that happened. But, you know, I talked to a few of the jurors on my podcast, and they could see the case and evidence for what we believed it proved. I don't know what would have changed their minds, if anything, and I don't know what we could have done differently to alter the outcome.

Q. Did you ever find and talk to the juror that thought that it was a conspiracy?

A. Yeah, he believed that there was something nefarious going on in the police department, and there was a possibility that things could have been planted or conspired against the killer. I don't find any evidence of that. Many people do find it unreasonable that an entire police force would band together to try and frame an innocent person or, as one said, maybe frame a guilty person when you have a mountain of evidence. There's no reason to continue to do that.

Q. Especially with the timeline, it's very bizarre how they would have had to go about planting that evidence

A. It just doesn't make any logical sense. They had no idea if the killer had an alibi. They didn't know if he was dead or alive. They had no idea about anything about him. But they were going to conspire to plant and frame him, and for why? They revered him. They loved him. They got autographs and pictures with him. Why would they do that? Why would they risk their careers, pensions, and reputations for what? It doesn't make any sense.

Q. Have you ever thought about having O.J. on your podcast?

A. Yeah. It was part of the process. The name of the show is *Confronting Him* (O.J.), and part of that is confronting him in theory too. So if he didn't end up being on, it's the process of confronting all of it. It's the case, trial, the witnesses, the grief, the domestic violence. It's the loss. It's the public perception. And if he was courageous enough to want to be able to sit down, then I was open to doing that.

Q. Didn't you try to see him once when he was in jail in Las Vegas?

A. I did. It was important for me to see him behind bars. The last time I saw him, we both walked out of a courtroom together, and so when he was put in prison or jail for the crimes that he had committed, I kind of wanted to shrink him in size to make it a little more manageable, the space that he was taking up in my brain. I pursued that pretty seriously, but I couldn't sign the contract they wanted me to, so it never happened.

Q. A nondisclosure contract?

A. Yes, his attorney at the time, we had a

couple of conversations. And I appreciated his candor with me. But in the end, he asked me to agree. The condition was that I would have to agree to sign a nondisclosure agreement, and I just wasn't willing to do that.

Q. That's kind of ridiculous because then he could have just said anything.

A. Of course, and that's why they wanted me to sign an agreement because they were concerned about that.

Q. What are your thoughts on O.J. and his social media rants on Twitter when he says that he's got people to get even with and things like that?

A. It's hard. Going back to what you said about the comment about moving on. It's very difficult to be going through my life as a single mom and business owner and have some sort of sense of new normality going on and then being harassed by that sort of nonsense. It's painful when he talks and his mannerisms. And all I'm looking at is the person who stabbed my brother to death. It's very hard to reconcile how those two things can happen in the same lifetime. It's gross. It's disgusting to me. But he is well within his rights to do it, and I can't stop that. I love that people go on and remind him constantly that he's a double murderer. I get some pleasure out of that.

Q. Did you know or meet O.J. before the crime happened?

A. No. I had no idea who he was.

Q. What are your thoughts on the death penalty?

A. I support the death penalty. I never used to because I was a psych background and thought everybody could be rehabilitated. But when this happened, I changed my mind. I do understand the flaws in the system. I don't support the death penalty as it stands today, but I do support its theory. I wished that we would tighten it up. I wished we could get better at it. I think it's just a waste of money to keep people on death row now. I don't think it carries the weight and the purpose behind it. But I certainly believe in the concept behind it.

Q. Would you be able to do it if you were given the button to push on O.J., could you do it?

A. 100 percent.

Q. 100 percent?

A. 100 percent. He brutally stabbed two people to death. He nearly decapitated his wife, and he stabbed my brother in the heart, his lungs, and his jugular vein. What he did to those two people that night is unforgivable and deserves to be met with the same torture.

Q. Especially because your family was thrust into the middle of something public. Your grief was public. The scene of...I just remember you and your father together when the verdict was read, and it just tore my heart out. I saw what it did to you and your family, and it was just heartbreaking.

A. I appreciate that. Loss is painful, and it looks different for everybody. Grief is different for everyone. I think what was different for us is we were doing it under the scrutiny of a country, and in some ways, that was great because it gave me an opportunity to share my big brother and to share my dad and our bond. And that's amazing because I am super proud of them, and I was raised by great people.

But in the same vein, it created a lot of emotion for a lot of people from the other side. There's been a lot of hate and anger towards us, and that's been hard to reconcile, too, because we were just kind of dumped off into this world that I didn't expect or couldn't prepare myself for. Not that anybody should ever. It's polarizing, and it's isolating. But for the most part, people have been very supportive and loving. And I'm grateful for that.

Q. What do you actually think happened on the night of the murders?

A. I think that my brother walked into a scene where Nicole was being attacked by the killer. I think he ran to try and stop it and got in the middle of it. And the killer pushed Nicole down on the step, and she hit her head and had a contusion on the back of her head. That's why we believe that. Then the killer attacked my brother and stabbed him. Five fatal wounds and over thirty defensive wounds, and they left him for dead. Then he went back and killed Nicole.

That's my belief. My brother was dropping off glasses that Nicole's mom had left at the restaurant where he worked and where Nicole and her family ate earlier in the evening. I know lots of people want to attach some kind of importance to my brother being the one to do that, but my brother had plans that night. And they were friends as far as I know, and that was the extent of that.

Q. Yes, there were lots of rumors going around saying that the two of them were having an affair.

A. She wasn't married. There's that little minor fact that doesn't make it an affair. But let's pretend they were. Let's pretend that they were in an intimate relationship, which doesn't warrant being stabbed to death.

Q. Now, you didn't know about the murder, did you? How long did it take before you knew about the murder?

A. So, the murders happened on June 12th. The news broke on the 13th. My dad had the notification made to him at about five o'clock on that Monday (June 13). So, it was on the news all day. My dad was a salesman at the time and in his car a lot. He had been listening to the news all day about Nicole Brown-Simpson and another person being stabbed to death in Brentwood. So, at about five o'clock, when he received a call from the coroner, that's when he was alerted. Within a couple of, maybe a minute, after them making that call to my dad, my brother's face was splashed all over the news. I did not hear until about 6:30 as I was working at the time and didn't get home until around 6:30. That's when my dad had told me.

Q. How did you deal with the verdict and the verdict celebrations when O.J. got off?

A. I hibernated a little bit. I think I went to the gravesite. I wanted to be with my brother. I felt very disappointed and betrayed by the system and by the jury. I was obviously shocked and angry. It didn't make any sense. It still doesn't make any sense to me on any level. However, I've gotten better at being able to understand it differently now. But it's hard that the person who stabbed my brother to death, whom I believe wholeheartedly did it and killed Nicole, has his freedom and is walking the streets. That is hard to reconcile, and I'm not any different than a lot of other families that have had the same experience or don't even have the opportunity to go to trial because their cases are cold.

Q. Now Johnny Cochrane has passed away since then, but he said something pretty awful after the verdict, didn't he?

A. I misspoke at one point in some interviews. He didn't say, "Gotcha." He looked at me, and he mouthed it. It's what I interpreted from the smirk that both he and O.J. had when they looked at me in the courtroom. He did not blurt it out. But again, we locked eyes. I know what the feeling is. I know what the insinuation is. They smirked at me, and then he mouthed it. That's my memory of it.

Q. When O.J. was arrested in Los Vegas and sent to jail, I think you said then that it took away a lot of your stress.

A. It did, but I don't think I realized how much. I was not burdened with some of that anxiety until he was released back because when he was released back, I felt anxious again, and I don't think I realized truly how much stress relief it was for him to be behind bars. But even from behind bars, he was able to create tension.

Q. Now, on your podcast *Confronting O.J. Simpson*, you've been able to meet a lot of the people who were involved in the trial, like Marcia Clark. Has meeting any of them changed your opinions of any of them from before?

A. No, I don't think it's changed my opinion. I believe the sole purpose for me was to have conversations with them and to get them to understand and extend some compassion. We were conjoined to this case, and I think each of us dealt with it differently, and how it manifested in our lives was interesting to me. We talked to Kato Kaylen. I know the world likes to look at him as a goofball, but he's just a down-to-earth guy that was sucked up into some things just like the rest of us and how it impacted his life. I know that he's gone on to do some fun things for himself from a professional standpoint. But it really impacted him. He had some death threats, you know, and he hibernated too. It's impacted his personal life deeply as it did with everybody that was involved in the case. That was a very important discussion to have with people. I think we forget the personal sacrifice.

Q. What about you? Have you ever had any threatening phone calls or emails from crazy people who support the killer?

A. All the time. I've certainly reported a number of threats because it's super scary to have people who can be so angry and to be so threatening. It's troublesome to me, but I understand it. I guess I understand it. I try to keep most of it at bay. Sometimes I can't help myself, but I engage sometimes because I'm human. It's harder for me when people go after my dad and brother. I don't let those go by without comments. But most of the time, I just know that it's somebody else's stuff. It's not about me. It's about them. If people have enough energy and time in their life that they could seek out a complete stranger to talk about hurting them or wishing violence upon them, then that's more about them than it is about me. And I need to leave that be.

Q. Now, you being a psych major and being trained in that field, do you think that O.J. ever had any remorse, or do you think that he actually believes the story that he's told? What would your professional opinion be of him as a killer?

A. I think he's a straight-up narcissist. I think that he is a psychopath, and I think that he doesn't have the ability to show remorse. I think that's been demonstrated by everything he's done. Even when he wrote the confession, *If I Did It,* there's no remorse in any of that or the interview that he did afterward talking about it. He is void of that, and that's quintessential psychopathic behavior. But I am not a killer. I am not a psychopath, so I don't know how you function in that world. But for someone who "claims" that he didn't do it, he certainly does not behave like a not guilty person. For someone who claims that he didn't do it, why doesn't he look for the person who did? Why isn't that important to him? Why isn't it important to him to get justice for his wife's murder? For his children, or for some random stranger who tried to save his wife's life? There's just nothing in his behavior for me to think that he's anything but guilty.

Q. With your podcast, do you feel that you achieved what you wanted to with it?

A. I think so. I'm still kind of decompressing, and we still have a few bonus episodes that are coming out. So, I still think I'm kind of in it. I'm trying to figure out what I'm still yearning for. But I think again, what was important for me was to talk to the people who were involved and to reiterate the truth and the facts behind them. I think there is a whole new generation of people who are learning about this case through a fictionalized lens, through conspiracy and cockamamie ideas about what happened that night, and it was important to me to try and lend a truthful narrative to the conversation because I think that it's been getting lost over the years. Also, to bring it back to survivors of domestic violence, grief, loss, and recovery. We don't like to talk about these things because it's not very sexy. I thought it was important to me to have an open dialogue, and that was the most important thing for me for the podcast.

Q. There's been so many shows, mini-series, or documentaries about the case. Have you seen any good representations of what happened that night and the trial?

A. No. I should say that from the fictionalized version, there have been lots of incredible documentaries that have been done. I'm all about the facts. I don't think dramatizing or fictionalizing something that was played out for the world to watch. I don't understand why that was done. It was done without the involvement of any of the people there. While I appreciate that the FX show, in some ways, painted a picture of his guilt, it was done in such a way that demeaned its importance of it. I mean, my brother and Nicole weren't even in it. It wasn't important for them to show the crime. How do you just dismiss that? The fact that they didn't talk to anybody involved in the case did a real disservice. But it is what it is.

Listen to the full interview with Kim Goldman on my website:

https://www.alanrwarren.com/hom-podcast-
episodes/episode/adcfcd9b/kim-
goldman-confronting-O.J.-simpson

Chapter 6
Who Killed Nicole?
Interview with Norman Pardo

O.J. Simpson & Norm Pardo

N ow that over twenty years have passed since the gruesome murders committed against Nicole Brown-Simpson and Ron Goldman that summer night, when most of the emotionally driven passion has slowly faded, we're left with the facts and what makes sense. It seems that most polls taken are still racially divided in whether a person believes that O.J. did it or not. I think most of the belief in a police conspiracy is gone even in modern times when conspiracy theories run amok. But there still are those who believe that Simpson did not commit these murders.

I think the best example I can use is by O.J.'s ex-manager Norm Pardo, as his belief was not rooted in Mark Fuhrman and a police set-up of Simpson. He just had a different suspect in mind. This is why I chose to run his interview as an example of someone who was on the inside of the Simpson family and business, who just honestly believed O.J. was innocent.

So, who is Norm Pardo? Pardo became O.J. Simpson's manager in 1999, and over the fifteen-year period of time that he worked with Simpson, he has collected well over seventy hours of film footage of Simpson and his family from behind the scenes, showing us things we wouldn't normally see. But it was from these videos that Pardo created a documentary movie called, *Who Killed Nicole* and released it to the public in 2019.

Previous to making this documentary, Pardo

also made another film called *O.J.: Made in America* in 2016.

The documentary bio, which would be followed by the book, claims that it will present shocking new evidence and testimony of the case which has never been seen before. So, is this just a way for Pardo to get some attention and make some money from the Simpson case? I can't answer that, but I can tell you that back when Regan Books published the book *If I Did It*, which was supposedly written by Simpson to explain that he didn't do it. Because if he had done it, this book tells you how he would have done it! That bio of the book in itself sounds crazy, and you can see why there was so much controversy over it. It was a crazy premise to explain how you would actually kill somebody, such as your wife or ex-wife, and the way you explained it proves that you couldn't have done it because the victim was killed in a different way.

Pardo was Simpson's manager during this time and was the one who set up the deal. Regan Books was to pay Simpson $600,000 for the book. And he didn't even have to write it. Instead, they brought in Pablo Fenjves, who had previously written some screenplays for Hollywood, to watch the Simpson trial, then ghostwrite the complete book without Simpson's involvement. Fenjves later claimed to have interviewed Simpson during the writing of this book, but he also believed that Simpson was a murderer.

In general, Pardo believes that Brown and Goldman were killed by a man called Glen Rogers, an employee of Dodi Fayed – the man who was dating Princess Diana until their death in a car accident back in 1997. So, what did Fayed have to do with Simpson?

Well, we decided to interview Pardo to see if there was anything that we could learn from him about this case that hadn't been brought up before. Could the murderer have been someone completely different than what we heard in court? Did the police ever look into other suspects?

Interview with Norman Pardo

This interview occurred in 2019, just after the film's release.

> Q. Norm, so how did you meet O.J., and how did you end up being his manager?
>
> A. My attorney introduced us. I just had taken my company public. I owned a dot com, and I was competing with Google. But my

company came up public before them. He introduced us at an airport hangar, which I had just purchased like a helicopter company. That's how we met.

Q. What kind of relationship did you guys have? Was it personal or business?

A. It was a little of both. I'm 100% business. I know that's me. That's what I do. But you have to get some personally involved with that because it's O.J. Simpson. But it was 90% business for me. But it was a little bit personal because I didn't want to lose, and I had a goal.

Q. What's your general view of O.J.? Did you like him? Was he a good person? How would you answer if someone asked what you thought of him?

A. He's a very likable person, and you have to like him. It's that way. If you don't like him, for example, we were at a restaurant once, and the guy across the way was giving him some mean looks. So, O.J. made it a point when he was going to the restroom and complimenting him on what a beautiful wife he had, etc. He was breaking the ice with him, and then before you knew it, the guy liked him. He senses when you don't like him, and he will actually try to correct the problem.

Q. He's a really charismatic guy. He seems to be able to spin stuff.

A. Yes. He's very good at it.

Q. What made you decide to make this documentary, and what were you hoping to get out of it?

A. Actually, the documentary was never going to come out, but everybody kept saying that I was going to do a documentary for twenty years. And so, I just wanted to know who killed Nicole. It wasn't about a documentary. I just spent twenty years hunting, looking, and digging to get the answers I wanted. It had nothing to do with anybody else. I didn't really, I don't mean to be mean, but I really didn't care what anybody else wanted. I just wanted to know for my own personal self who killed Nicole. I knew that the way everyone was positioning it, it was either O.J. or O.J., but after meeting him for a while, I knew that there was more to the story than just O.J. killing her.

It actually wasn't me that started it. It was Kyle Saylor, out of Nashville, who contacted me, probably six years ago and kept hounding me to let them produce the movie *The Saylor Brothers*. Last year, I told them, "Let's do it." Here's everything I got, and there were boxes and boxes of stuff. I think I blew their minds. There are terabytes of information. They had no idea of the amount of money. You know I spent more than three-quarters of a million dollars, and the amount of time I spent, to find out who killed Nicole. My investigation was more thorough than they did in L.A.

Q. Why do you think that is? Why didn't the prosecution do as much as you did?

A. I think they got themselves into a situation where they had to go the route that they were going. When they first arrested O.J., he was the killer, and it was rage. They sold that story to America. Then, when they found out that there were other people involved, they couldn't go back and say, "Well, he was raging, but he hired this guy, and everybody worked together." So they had to do what they had to do. There was really know no way around it.

Q. During your documentary, you say that O.J. wasn't the jealous type. Can you explain that?

A. Well, when we were out there, he would have a girlfriend, and he would give the girlfriend to other guys, and he didn't really care. He wasn't the jealous kind. He was more of a player. I didn't see O.J. get jealous of any of his girlfriends. The one in Miami, he caught her with, I guess, a whole football team and still stayed with her. He used to call me and say, "Norm, if she called you, you just tell her I'm with you because I don't want to deal with her this week."

Q. You also say that his relationship with the Kardashians is what set this whole thing into motion. What was their relationship like?

A. The relationship with Robert was good at first. Robert gave O.J. a lot. I was amazed when we started digging into how much he really did for O.J. During the start of Kardashian's career with Radio and Records (a trade publication), he was one of the original owners. He gave O.J. a share of that business, a big chunk of it. There were only three owners when it started, and O.J. was one of them that Robert brought in, along with his brother. So, he brought him into a lot of things that helped him. Then, of course, it got sour when O.J. took everything away from

Robert. Robert gave him everything that O.J. had, and O.J. took everything away from Robert.

Q. You also say, allegedly, O.J. slept with Kris Jenner too?

A. I have to say, allegedly, anytime you say anything with Kardashian. Kardashian has been my biggest problem. I mean, the entire world is so afraid of them right now. I mean, I got this straight from the top brass at the big networks. Because if my movie talks about them in any way, shape or form, they don't even want to talk about my movie. They're cute, though. They watched the movie and say, "Oh my God, this is the definitive story, but we can't air it," which made me laugh. So, I asked, "Why can't you air it?" I responded, "Well, Robert's dead." "It doesn't matter. You know how much power the Kardashian's wielded right now." So, basically, I am banned in America, but we're doing much better now as I am talking with a Canadian network that wants to air my movie. So, in other countries, I'm good. We're just banned in America because of the Kardashians right now.

Q. So, in your movie, it sounds like you are saying that O.J. didn't do it. Or are you saying that he was behind it?

A. Therein lies the problem. That's the hardest thing I have to solve. Did he hire Glen Rogers to go over there? Or did Robert Kardashian hire Glen Rogers? That's the one thing neither one of them would talk about. Now, Glen Rogers' son called me and claimed that it was Robert. By the way, Glen Rogers had called him and wanted to know how I found out what happened that night. He called me from prison. Glen Rogers is on death row right now in Florida.

Right now, I thought we would stop, so I can tell you who Glen Rogers is if you're not aware. Glen Rogers is an American serial killer given the handles "Cross Country Killer" and "The Casanova Killer." He was suspected of killing one older man and four women. When he confessed, he claimed to have killed around 70 people in total. Later, he recanted his confession and said that he was only joking.

Rogers's brother Clay was in a documentary in 2012 called *My Brother the Serial Killer*, where, according to Clay, before the murders, Rogers had met Nicole. After that meeting, Clay said Glen told him, "I'm going to take her down."

Q. Can you talk about Glen Rogers, who he was, and how he got involved in these murders?

A. Glen Rogers is a bonafide serial killer. He killed a guy named Mark Peters, and then, after he killed him in Ohio, I think it was, he went from there to California. He was already wanted for killing Peters. But he took Peters's identification and his social security number and everything and was working under the name of Mark Peters.

That's why a lot of people can't place him at the scene of the crime because he was going under the name Mark Peters and not Glen Rogers. So, when they did a couple of other documentaries, they said there was no way he could do it because he wasn't in town at the time. But he was. We know this because we have the W2 forms from his employer that stated Mark Peters was working for him. Mark Peters actually admitted working right after the day Nicole died. The reason I got all of this stuff is that Glen Rogers gave it to me himself.

Q. How did he get involved in the murders of Nicole and Ron Goldman?

A. From what I'm understanding, he was hired to just watch Nicole. Just like the other gentleman was hired. There was a guy named William Wasz, who was the first guy hired to follow Nicole and find out who was dealing drugs, etc. Then, it switched over because that guy got arrested. He was actually arrested in Paula Barbieri's car (O.J. Simpson's girlfriend at the time of the murders) with a .22 caliber pistol, Nicole's diary with her whereabouts in it, a crack pipe, and something else.

In his testimony, he claimed that O.J. or Robert told him where to pick up Paula Barbieri's car, etc. etc. I thought that was a great clue because that put the odds of somebody stealing Paula Barbieri's car and getting into an accident in her car with Nicole's whereabouts in it a billion to one without somebody being a part of it, either Robert or O.J.

Q. What do you think Robert's motive would be for having Nicole killed?

A. Honestly, I don't think any of them knew the killings were going to happen to be honest. I think that at the time, I know Robert was mad because of that whole affair with Kris. But I don't think anybody knew the killing was going to happen. I think the killing happened because it was going to be basically a thug down of Ron Goldman, and they didn't expect it to go the way it went. That's why people got hurt.

O.J. was the first one cut. That's why the blood went from the crime scene all the way to his house. He was cut by Ron. Ron was the first person to pull a knife. It wasn't Glen. Glen just took the knife away from him and killed him with it.

Q. Well, what was happening there at the time? Do you suggest that Ron Goldman was selling drugs or something like that?

A. Yes. Ron Goldman was the drug dealer that was dealing drugs and pulling Nicole into it. Not realizing that it was sort of the reverse. So, they thought they'd just go over and thug down Ron. And that would be the end of it, and Ron would leave it all alone. But when Ron got pushed into the bushes, he fought back. That's what happened. I think that's honestly the only thing that could have happened.

The way that O.J. was cut, he was cut on the outside of his finger. He wasn't cut on the inside of his finger, and when O.J. puts his finger in your face, that's what he did to me thousands of times that same thing. He points it in your face like he's yelling at you. That's what he does. I think that when Ron pulled out the knife, he cut him in that same finger. And O.J. ran home like a baby, which is what he would do, and left Glen there with Ron.

That's why Glen got so mad because he wasn't paid to do that. He was paid to go over there and be a backup thug, and he got lured into something that he wasn't paid for. Nicole and Ron were actually killed two hours apart from each other. They weren't killed at the same time. We also proved that in our movie.

Q. So, when he killed Goldman and threw him in the bushes, what made him go and kill Nicole? Why wouldn't he have just left then?

A. Well, what happened was that O.J. had already left him there, and he got mad. He said he grabbed up one of the gloves and said, "The n-word wasn't going to leave me holding the bag." Then, he ran over and threw it over his fence. That's how the glove got over O.J.'s fence. Then, he ran over to the back of the house, and he was going to leave. But then he thought, okay, he didn't get paid. So, he called Nicole and told her that he would have some nose sugar for her. He said that he did that so that when she came to the door, she would have money on her. He went back to get that. Figuring that he was going to get paid. So, when she came to the door, he told her, "Let's do this around the corner." They went around the corner where Ron was, and he just got up behind her, slit her throat, took the money, and that was it. And her jewelry, and then he said he pawned the jewelry in Vegas or Nevada somewhere.

Q. Have you talked with O.J. since doing this film?

A. No, he's really mad at me right now. He's one of those kinds of people that says, "I didn't have nothing to do with it. You don't want to know what happened. Just let it go." That's what he's always told me. He should have told me, "I didn't do anything." Instead, he didn't do that. He said, "You don't want to know what happened. Let it go."

So, I knew he knew. The problem is that he's never been tried on conspiracy. He was only tried for the murders. So, he could be retried, and that's why I think he doesn't want anything to come out. I'm not mad at him. I just had to know.

Q. Has he said anything to you about it? Or has he done any media to respond to it?

A. No. He won't talk about it. That's how O.J. works. If he wants something to go away, he just shuts up. Then it'll go away. He does that with anybody who gets him riled up. He just won't talk about it. And by not talking about it, then they don't get his side. And it usually just goes away. But in reality, it doesn't make him look that bad. I mean, he wasn't there during either killing. I mean, he left before Ron was killed. They had already started fighting, but he did leave. He never went back for Nicole because she was killed an hour and a half after he was on the plane going to Chicago.

Q. What does the Goldman family say about your theory?

A. I got a lot of pushback because you don't ever say the victim was anything more than a victim. But Ron was into a lot of things. All of his files are sealed because they said he was an informant. You can't open up Ron Goldman's files. So, he was into a lot of things. Just like Glen Rogers's files are all sealed as he was an informant.

Q. Whom were they informing for, and what were they doing?

A. Well, what we can most figure out was that it was drug related because they were both dealing with drug people. Glen Rogers, in one of his letters, stated that's how he used to get away with things. He was an informant. If somebody was to get killed, he would just say, "Oh, I'll tell you," and he would just point at somebody and say, "He did it." As an informant, he would just have to testify against them.

Q. What's been the general feedback on your documentary?

A. People just can't believe how much was hidden. Everybody who downloads that video has watched it four or five times which is incredible. You can't grasp it the first time. The first time you'll see a lot of stuff in it, but the second time you'll say, I didn't notice that.

Q. What about O.J.'s suicide note?

A. Everyone thought that the suicide note

was written by O.J., but we compared all of the signatures, and there's no way O.J. Simpson wrote that suicide note. It wasn't his handwriting. It wasn't his signature. It was actually written by someone that was more of a child. Robert turned it in.

Q. Who do you think wrote it then?

A. Well, I can't mention any of the Kardashian children. But Robert Kardashian is the one who turned in the suicide note. But when you look at the signature, just look at the signature at the bottom of the suicide note. It's not even close. I've got probably one hundred of O.J.'s signatures, and I brought them all up, and not one of them even come close. The suicide note actually put a smiley face inside the signature. O.J. would never put a smiley face inside his signature. So, whoever it was, was a child. It makes you wonder. I would like to know if any of the Kardashian family would know who signed that note. It would be interesting to find that out.

Q. Have you asked any of the Kardashians about it?

A. No, they won't talk to me. They're mad at

me because of the alleged Kris Jenner affair with O.J. I guess I could have left that out, but there has to be a motive, and that's something that would make Robert mad. You have to find out if there's a reason why Robert would be mad. Would he have a motive? So, I had to look for a motive in him. We looked at four different people that we tried to find if there was a motive for any of them. Robert is actually the only one who came out with a lot of negatives. Between that situation that happened, which could have been a trigger. If you look at the photograph taken with all of the Kardashians with O.J. Simpson and Nicole, I think it was on April 1st, just before the murders. If you look at that photograph that was taken just weeks before the murder, you'll see that all the families were together. All the Kardashians, all the Jenners, and all the Simpsons. Except for one person, that was Robert Kardashian. He's the only one missing from that photograph.

What really gets me, and the thing that makes me most angry about this whole thing? It wasn't O.J. Simpson or Nicole Brown or anything. I mean, honestly, that whole situation was a sad state of affairs, but none of them were great people. They all had problems. They were all doing stuff that they shouldn't be doing. The only innocent victims in all of this were the people that Glen Rogers killed after this. That was the innocent people. There were four victims after this happened that he killed, and after the prosecutor interviewed him about the possibility of him being a murderer.

It's after O.J.'s attorney interviewed him. O.J.'s attorney interviewed Glen Rogers and said Glen Rogers couldn't possibly be the one. The prosecutor interviewed Glen Rogers and said no, there's no possible way for him to be the one. If you think about that, Glen Rogers was already on the federal Most Wanted List, the F.B.I.'s Most Wanted List for killing Mark Peters. So, why did the prosecutor interview him and then let him go? He wouldn't have gone on to kill four more people. That's why he's on death row right now. It wasn't four people before killing Nicole. It was from after. Those people would still be alive right now if the prosecutor didn't hustle him and get them out of town.

They did not want anybody to come up and say, "O.J. didn't do it," because that would throw out their entire thing. You can't bring Glen Rogers into the mix. That's why all of the

files we wanted, one of them we had our hands-
on, and it was six inches thick, and then when
they finally released it, it was six pages.

Q. What are your thoughts on Marcia Clark and
the prosecution of the case?

A. The prosecutors had to know that all of
this stuff was going on. I mean, you can't hide it
from everybody. I don't blame them, but I'm
saying that what they did was wrong. Somebody
did a lot of bad things, like the planting of the
blood on the gate and the planting of the blood
on the socks. It would have been good enough
to get O.J. from the crime scene with the blood
drops that went from the crime scene to his
house that didn't have the preservative in it.

But, when they put the blood on the glove
and socks, you had preservatives in it, and so all
the blood drops ended up being thrown out. So,
by trying to make it look like more than what it
was, it made it worse.

Q. Was Fuhrman behind that?

A. Well, there was a lot of blood that was
missing, so somebody was. I mean some of the
blood in the Bronco. I mean, we were able to
knock those shoes out in a minute. They did that

whole trial based on the Bruno Magli shoes. That was the big thing, the Bruno Magli shoe prints all over the crime scene. The only problem with the Bruno Magli shoes being all over the crime scene was the shoe print inside the Bronco. When they had an FBI shoe specialist and tire print specialist on the stand to testify, they asked him if the show print in the Bronco matched the shoe prints at the scene of the crimes. He was very adamant when he said no. So, if the shoe prints found in the Bronco were Bruno Maglis, then they weren't on O.J.'s feet. In fact, the shoe prints in the Bronco were from tennis shoes. So what did O.J. change into bloody tennis shoes on his way into the Bronco? Which explains a lot. You see, O.J. left before the blood was everywhere. That's why his shoe print wasn't what it was supposed to be because it's just his footprint with his own blood. He was the one dripping blood because he got his finger cut. But, he left before the big murders happened.

That's why the lady who was walking his dog back home, the couple who found his dog, said there were no dead bodies out there at 10:30. They were right because Nicole wasn't there yet. Ron was dead, but he was up in the bushes, so there was no blood on the sidewalk from somebody being killed in the bushes. The blood on the sidewalk all came from Nicole, and she didn't die until 11:30 or 12 o'clock. That's why everybody else said they never saw bodies until then.

Q. Did O.J. not know that Glen Rogers killed both Nicole and Ron? I mean, he wrote that book *If I Did It,* and there's no mention of it.

A. Well yeah, he knew who did it. But he didn't really write that book. They came to him with that book and said here's the deal. We'll give you so much cash, and you say you don't dispute that you wrote the book. He called me and said that's what they told me. So, he didn't know what was in the book.

Q. He didn't think the book was going to hurt his reputation.

A. He didn't care. He told me that people who think I'm a murderer are going to think that I'm a murderer, but you'd take the money to Norm. I was like, this is not a good thing. And that was sort of the beginning of our separation. Because I said that's not a good thing to do because the whole book thing doesn't make sense.

O.J. Simpson cannot be sued by anybody for anything. The publisher of his book would not take $600,000 and put it into his bank account because the judgment against him from the civil suit would just take it. So, they had to give him $600,000 in cash in a suitcase because there was no way he could put it in a bank account. They would not give O.J. $600,000 in cash and say go write us a book, because O.J. wouldn't write it.

They would never get their money back because they couldn't sue him. So, they just took the cash over there with the book and said, "Now, you don't dispute that you wrote this book, and we'll give you this suitcase." That's how it went down. I mean, I think he had to read the book because he had to do the interview about the book and had to know what was in it. The book was written by a guy who was walking his dog. He was one of the people who was involved in the first trial.

Q. What can you tell me about the Goldmans as you mention them in your book too?

A. Yes, we investigated them as well because

you have to investigate everybody. I needed to know what their affiliations were with different people. The more we investigated them, the more we found that they don't have a really squeaky clean background, no more than anybody else does. Fred Goldman is married to a lady named Patty Glass. Everybody can google this. Marty Glass was Patty Glass' husband and also part of a 100 million dollar cocaine smuggling ring in Chicago. They got busted, and he was on trial when Fred Goldman ran away with her to California. So, he was already on trial for being a cartel member somewhat. So, they have a direct connection to that.

Q. So, that's why you think Ron Goldman was selling drugs?

A. I think he was, but I don't think he was a dealer. He didn't have the finances to be the dealer. You had to have somebody else with more money. Ron Goldman was on his way to a marina that night when he left the restaurant. He wasn't going there just to drop off glasses. He was going to drop off the glasses on the way to the marina. Nobody figured out how he got from the restaurant to Nicole's house.

There was no car. There were a bunch of

rumors that they found a car, but there was no car. So, the question was, how was he going to get from there to the marina as it was a two-and-a-half-hour walk to the marina from the restaurant? There's no way that Ron Goldman said I'm going to drop off these glasses at Nicole's on my way to walking a two-and-a-half-hour walk to the marina. I mean, he wouldn't be there until about two in the morning.

So, he had a ride. He had transportation from the restaurant to Nicole's house. Now, if that's a good friend of his and oh my God, Ron's being killed, a friend would at least call the police, wouldn't he? If it was a taxicab, would he just drive off and say, "I'm not getting involved in this?" So, what happened to his transportation? Whoever was driving the car, where did he go? It took a while for me to figure that one out. The only way that the transportation wouldn't be part of the trial somewhere saying, "I saw him go in there or something," is if that person was participating.

I know that Glen Rogers was already getting close to Nicole and Ron. So, I would think that in my gambling that Glen Rogers picked Ron up from the restaurant and took him to Nicole's house. That's why when Ron went through the gate, Glen Rogers was behind him and O.J. was in front of him, already there. But that's the only logical way Ron made it over to Nicole's going to the marina. Nobody walks that far.

Q. So, Nicole never heard them attacking Goldman? Was she not at home?

A. She was at home. The way the house was set up, her bedroom and the kid's bedroom were on the other end. It's like a long, skinny apartment. So, all of the bedrooms are on the other end of the house. Totally opposite to the end where all the violence took place. So, she would have never even heard what was going on out there.

Q. What was Glen Rogers's relationship with Nicole?

A. Well, he claimed that he was dating her in all of the letters that we got. He did have pictures of him and Nicole, but the FBI took those pictures. We can't seem to get those pictures back. I saw them, but I haven't been able to see them since the FBI took them.

So, there are pictures of Glen and Nicole out a couple of nights earlier at a club with Dodi

Fayed. Luckily, we did get a witness that night with them that came forward. I was lucky being the O.J. guy (manager) because anybody who knew anything about it would call me up and say, "I've got this, I've got that."

Q. What was Dodi Fayed's connection with Nicole and O.J.?

A. Well, I didn't know where it was going either, to be honest. I just thought it was very interesting that Dodi was with Nicole and Glen a few nights before. So, I don't know.

Listen to the full interview with Norman Pardo on my website:

https://www.alanrwarren.com/
hom-podcast-episodes/
episode/cd926ee0/norman-
pardo-who-killed-nicole

Chapter 7
Las Vegas Arrest
Interview with Andy Caldwell

O.J. Simpson would not only remain in the spotlight after both trials but also get arrested and charged with breaking the law again. Only this time, things wouldn't end so well for him.

It started on the evening of September 13, 2007, when Simpson and a group of his friends went to a hotel room in the Palace Station located in Las Vegas. What was supposed to be a simple buying of memorabilia turned out to be a strong-armed robbery.

O.J. Simpson had heard from a friend of his, Tom Riccio, who was a sports memorabilia collector, that he knew of someone in Las Vegas who had a lot of Simpson's memorabilia. Under the impression that it was stolen from him, Simpson devised a plan to have Riccio arrange a meeting between him and the person who had the memorabilia so he could purchase some of it. Riccio didn't tell the dealer that Simpson was the buyer.

Simpson had gone to Las Vegas to go to a wedding, and after he attended the pre-wedding dinner, he got five friends who were also attending the wedding to join him as he went to the hotel to meet the memorabilia dealer. Simpson and his group got to room 1203 of the Palace Station by 7:30 p.m. that evening for the meeting.

As soon as they entered the hotel room, Simpson ordered his friends not to let anyone leave the room until he said it was okay. An argument began between the memorabilia dealer and Simpson, who accused the dealer of stealing the items. During the argument, one of Simpson's gang threatened to use a gun on the dealer. The other members of Simpson's party grabbed the pillowcases from the pillows on the beds and started to put all of the memorabilia, over 1000 items, in them. Within about six minutes, Simpson and his group removed all of the memorabilia from the dealer and returned to the hotel where they were staying, the Palms Casino Resort.

The police were notified by the memorabilia dealer later that evening that he had been robbed and named Simpson as the primary suspect in the crime. The following day, the police questioned Simpson but let him go. During that conversation with detectives, Simpson named the other people who had gone to the hotel room with him. That led to detectives arresting Walter Alexander and charging him with two counts of robbery with a deadly weapon, one count of conspiracy to commit a robbery, two counts of assault with a deadly weapon, and one count of burglary using a deadly weapon. Police also searched Alexander's home, finding two guns they believed were used during the robbery.

The following day, September 16th, Simpson was arrested as well. Police recovered a recording taken in the hotel room during the robbery. The recording device was put there by Simpson's friend Riccio, who later claimed that he planted it in the room to get a recording to prove that the memorabilia dealer had stolen Simpson's property. Instead, the recording just helped prove that Simpson and his gang took the memorabilia by force. It must be said that Riccio was given immunity by the District Attorney for both giving law enforcement the tapes and testifying for the prosecution.

Almost immediately, Simpson was interviewed by the *Los Angeles Times,* saying, "I'm O.J. Simpson. How am I going to think that I'm going to rob somebody and get away with it? Besides, I thought about what happens in Vegas and stays in Vegas. You've got to understand. This ain't somebody going to steal somebody's drugs or something like that. This is somebody going to get his private belongings back. That's not a robbery."

While Simpson was trying to spin his tale to the public, the hidden recording of the incident was released to the public, which began to tell a different story. The sections of the tape where

Simpson said, "Don't let nobody out of this room," and "Motherfucker, you think you can steal my shit and sell it?" were played over and over again on every news platform there was.

To make things worse for Simpson, Walter Alexander began talking to the press. Alexander believed that the whole case was just a setup by Riccio to get Simpson. When detectives interrogated Alexander, he claimed that it was Simpson's idea to bring guns along with them to the hotel room. He added that Simpson just wanted to have the guns to scare them and not actually to use them on the dealer. Alexander was also given a deal by the prosecution allowing him to plead guilty to a lesser offense if he testified against Simpson. Another of Simpson's accomplices, Charles Cashmore, also agreed to testify against Simpson for a lesser offense.

Alexander's statement also claimed that another person was with them in the hotel room and was a part of Simpson's gang. A guy named McClinton pretended to be a police officer and acted over-the-top tough, which Simpson hadn't asked him to do. This apparently surprised everyone, and Simpson supposedly had to tell him to take it easy and to calm down.

At Simpson's hearing, bail was set at

$125,000, and he was ordered not to speak to any of his co-defendants. He also had to surrender his passport. Simpson was charged with conspiracy to commit a crime, conspiracy to commit kidnapping, conspiracy to commit a robbery, burglary while in possession of a deadly weapon, first-degree kidnapping with use of a deadly weapon for Bruce Fromong, first-degree kidnapping with use of a deadly weapon for Alfred Beardsley, robbery with the use of a deadly weapon for Bruce Fromong, robbery with use of a deadly weapon for Alfred Beasley, assault with a deadly weapon for Bruce Fromong, assault with a deadly weapon for Alfred Beasley, coercion with a deadly weapon for Bruce Fromong, and coercion with a deadly weapon for Alfred Beasley. On all twelve counts, he did not enter a plea.

When Simpson was released, he headed for his home in Miami, Florida. Simpson would go on to break his parole by talking with a co-defendant, so he was arrested again and sent back to Nevada for another hearing to answer for these new charges. Bail was doubled to $250,000, which he came up with, and he returned to his home in Miami once again.

He returned to Nevada again to face trial on September 8, 2008. The trial lasted under one month and ended with Simpson being convicted on all charges. He was remanded in custody until he was sentenced. On December 5, 2008, Simpson was sentenced to serve eight of the ten counts concurrently with a minimum of nine years and a maximum sentence of 33 years with the possibility for parole after serving nine years. Simpson served his time at the Lovelock Correctional Center in Lovelock, Nevada.

Simpson's parole hearing took place live on television with coverage from all major cable networks. During the hearing, Simpson would say things like he had lived a conflict-free life. The four parole board members voted unanimously in favor of Simpson being released, saying they believed he was at low risk of re-offending. Simpson would be granted parole on July 20, 2017, and was released on October 1, 2017, after serving nine years in prison at the age of seventy.

Andy Caldwell is one of the detectives that questioned and arrested O.J. Simpson for the robbery. He wrote a book, *Room 1203: O.J. Simpson's Las Vegas Conviction*, covering his experiences with Simpson, and agreed to discuss it on our show. Caldwell has since retired from the Las Vegas Metropolitan Police Department and now works as a Pastor in the Mill City Christian church in Oregon.

Caldwell faced verbal abuse from Simpson's attorney at the time, LaVergne, with statements like, "Andy Caldwell's a big, fat, lying piece of shit." This was after Caldwell made a few statements about what he saw when he went to Simpson's hotel room to question him about the reported robbery.

"His girlfriend was in the room running around chasing a little white dog that she was trying to put a sweater on. He was yelling at her that she needed to leave. The room has about eight to ten detectives in it. He sits on the corner of the bed, and I sat in front of him. We were waiting for his lawyer to show up, so nobody was asking him anything about the case. Suddenly he looked at me and, after a couple of minutes, said, "Hey, did you take my phone?" It caught me off guard, but then my partner, Eddie, stepped up and told him his phone was in between his legs. He looked down, and as soon as he saw his phone, he grabbed it, pulled it up to his chest, and suddenly threw himself backward onto his bed. He started wiggling around with his arms and legs up in the air. He did this for about 15 or

20 seconds before he sat back up and acted as if nothing happened."

LaVergne continued his attack on Caldwell, "All of this is bullshit. This is bullshit. They're trying to make it like Simpson was in a delusional state making all these wild, kind of crazy remarks, and he wasn't doing any of that stuff. Andy Caldwell's a fucking loser. That's that. He just happens to be a cop that was trying to capitalize on O.J. Simpson's fame. Mr. Simpson was cooperative with all of the detectives at all phases."

Caldwell says he has no ill will towards Simpson or his attorney. The strange thing is hearing an attorney go public with such crass comments is not only unprofessional, but it's also something you never see.

The Summer of 2017 not only brought Caldwell's book to the public but also an A&E two-hour documentary special called *Guilty: The Conviction of O.J. Simpson,* which follows detective Caldwell's story about the state of mind Simpson had during that period of time. A&E also ran a documentary earlier focusing on the tape recordings of Simpson during the hotel robbery in Las Vegas called *O.J. Speaks: The Hidden Tapes.*

Interview with Andy Caldwell

This interview took place in the fall of 2017.

Q. How did this case fall into your lap, to begin with?

A. It fell into my lap because, at the time, I was a robbery detective in Las Vegas, and the robbery occurred in my area of responsibility.

Q. But were you surprised? How did they call because it's not like he was robbed? He robbed someone else.

A. When we got that call and were told that it was O.J. Simpson, I think we laughed. It's absurd. You think about what he's got away with in the past. Why would he come to Las Vegas and commit a crime? So, we laughed.

Q. So, were you skeptical at first, or did you think we've got to go and get this guy? What was your feeling?

A. Yeah, you know, really skeptical at first. After we got our laugh—and we did, we got our laughs—then we had to go there and find out why these people are calling and trying to say that they got robbed at gunpoint by O.J.

Simpson and a few other men. So, it wasn't until we actually got there that my partner and I went up to look at the surveillance video and saw that O.J. Simpson really was there. Initially, we were thinking that our victims may not have been in touch with reality. It took a while for us to be convinced.

Q. I guess you get a lot of that in Las Vegas because everyone is trying to be famous. So it must keep you on your guard.

A. It does, yes, because, in Vegas, you do have them (celebrities) coming and going quite a bit. So you never know what calls are going to be really involving a celebrity or not.

Q. So, you went up to his room, and I enjoyed the encounter that you had with him. Maybe talk about that when you first came to the room and knocked on the door and came in. How was he to you as police?

A. You know, I think what's kind of telling here is, you know, just like he was going to find the real murderer, he wanted to partner up with me, help me get to the bottom of what I had to investigate. So, he was incredibly welcoming. We didn't intentionally go into the interview at his hotel room with ten detectives. We were just going to go in with three. But when we went to his hotel room, he invited everyone in and was just over the top friendly.

Given the moment, you can't blame the guys who weren't supposed to go in because O.J. waved them in and said, "Hey, come on in, guys." So, everybody came into the room. His personality is a little overwhelming at first, and I write about it a little bit in the book. There is a moment when you are starstruck by the man. Fame, infamy, whatever it is, when you stand right there in front of him, his personality is dynamic and outgoing, and you get caught up in the moment.

Q. So, did he ask to speak to a lawyer?

A. He actually called us and asked for an interview. So, he actually already arranged and made clear that he had a lawyer. However, when we got there, his lawyer wasn't present. So, we're still bound by the rules of Miranda, and he invoked his rights. When we got there, he told us his lawyer was coming, and that's when he invited us all in to wait for the lawyer. He made all sorts of statements, unsolicited, that implicated him in the crime because he likes to talk. That's where we had our moment where we had a room with about ten detectives standing around him, and he sat on the corner of his bed, and my partner and I were right in front of him, and he was playing with his phone in his hand. That's when the moment happens that I'll never forget. He sat his phone down between his legs, sitting on the corner of the bed. He continued to talk to me for a few moments. Then he looked kind of lost. Then he accused me of stealing his phone, and he caught me a little off guard. Luckily, my partner said, "Mr. Simpson, it's between your legs." When O.J. reached down and grabbed that phone, and then he caressed it on his chest and then threw himself backward on the bed and started laughing. Then he started putting his hands, arms, and legs up into the air and wiggled on the bed. Here we stood, all these detectives in the room, not knowing what we were looking at. This went on for about twenty seconds which might initially seem like a short time, but it was really a long time of quietness as we watched this man do this. Then he sat right down again and continued talking as if it didn't happen.

Q. Do you think he did that on purpose in case they found him guilty? Somehow he could claim he had a mental issue going on at the time.

A. No, I actually think that he lived in his own world. And in his world, that's completely normal behavior. And he expects it to be normal for anyone who witnesses it. As you deal with him more often, you begin to realize that he's in a completely different world.

Q. That almost sounds like he's on drugs.

A. Well, he did have erratic behavior, which is consistent with someone who was under the influence of some sort of controlled substance. What that is, I can't tell you. Another thing that struck me was that he was wearing the exact same clothes as he was the day before. It kind of steps you back into that moment that this is just another bad guy that I investigate who is a criminal, a crook, a street thug committing crimes. That helps me bring it back and not be star-struck.

Q. Does O.J. have that same ability to charm people who are not fans of him and his sport's history?

A. I think this guy has an inherent ability to

charm people, and I think he manipulates that for his own benefit and gain, whatever the circumstances. You know, we had all of these audio recordings of him interacting with people before and after the robbery. You see his ability to shift from memorabilia dealers to his kind of thug codependent pseudo-law enforcement. So, you see, this kind of chameleon-like personality caters to each individual person to manipulate them for his own benefit. So, yeah, I think that even those outside of sports fans and movie fans, he still has that kind of ability to charm them.

Q. Did you consider his ability to change personalities really just a sociopathic behavior, as they quite often don't have real emotions and only mimic the emotions that they've learned from watching others?

A. I tell you, that was one thing that was definitely noticeable about him. There were audio recordings that we had leading up to and planning the incident that revealed the character trait he has. You know, sitting at a bar with a bunch of friends that he's planning a crime with, it's very different than when he interacted with law enforcement, very different than how he interacted when we saw him in court, or when you saw him at a parole hearing. He does transform very easily, and he appeals to his audience.

Q. I'm sure he got used to carousing with people from being a star for so many years too.

A. Sure, and I believe there's this expectation he had that everybody would do what he wanted them to. Part of the reason the bail bondsman revoked his bail, and he ended up back in jail, part of that reason was that he was trying to manipulate witnesses through the bail bondsman. He was asking the bail bondsman to call co-defendants and ask him (the bail bondman) to tell them (co-defendants) messages from O.J. to the co-defendants, which he is not supposed to do. Clearly, we have a voicemail, and he expects that to happen. There was no 'this might happen.' There was an expectation that you 'will do this.' Luckily, the bail bondsman had the integrity to say no. It was certainly a violation of the parole as he was not allowed to have any conversations with any of the co-defendants. O.J.'s expectation was that everybody believed what he just said regardless of its actual truth.

Q. Did O.J. actually carry a gun himself during this crime?

A. No, we never established that he had a gun. But what we had was, and this is one of those misrepresentations that he made at his parole hearing, that he consistently stuck with his story and that he never knew that there was a gun. There was an audio recording that we had that was very poor quality, but it occurred after the robbery happened. During this recording, O.J. Simpson's heard saying to his codefendant, "Hey, you never pulled that piece out in the hall, right?" and the codefendant says, "no, no, no, no." O.J. then says, "Well, when they look at the video, they'll have nothing then."

Q. That is straight coaching.

A. Yes, and that audio recording was so wonderful because it was the strongest piece of evidence to corroborate what the witnesses said that he asked them to bring firearms and that there were, in fact, firearms in the room. But O.J. has consistently said that there were no guns or that he saw no guns. It's so absurd that it's hard to believe. But once you get to see and know his personality, he lives in this alternate world. Truth doesn't matter to him. What he creates, he expects you to believe.

Q. He might have gotten away with one of the biggest crimes in history.

A. Well, according to his parole hearing, he said that he's never been accused of using a weapon against anybody.

Q. And he also said that he's never been violent!

A. But I think that's what made the case so fascinating. One of my biggest gripes, the reason that I wrote the book, is because I always fear these kinds of storylines of his – he steals his own stuff back and that it really wasn't a crime. In all actuality, it wasn't his own property. And it was a crime. If people give my book a chance, they'll find out that this was a really violent encounter. It was a crime that he committed, and he deserves to go to prison for what he did.

Q. Can you give us a rundown of the crime for the listeners who don't know what happened? What was O.J. arrested and sent to jail for?

A. There was a memorabilia dealer in

Southern California named Tom Riccio who was aware of some family heirlooms that were floating around out there that belonged to O.J. Simpson at one time. Tom Riccio was aware that Simpson had just lost the rights to the book he wrote, *If I Did It,* and he was no longer going to get any proceeds from that book.

So, Tom Riccio was able to manipulate O.J. Simpson's emotions and get him into a contract to exclusively sign some of those books for him. In return, Tom Riccio was going to connect him with his family heirlooms. That was the initial plan, but it all fell apart. So, O.J. Simpson probably thought there were going to be different items in that room than what was actually there.

So, when the family heirlooms kind of fall apart, there's a last-minute fill-in of "Hey, let's just bring some O.J. memorabilia, and maybe that'll work," and O.J. will sign the books for him. O.J. decided to do a little side planning and contacted some men to come with him to do security and bring guns, and they were just going to steal the property back. That's where it all fell apart.

So, the property in the hotel room in Las Vegas was not what he thought it was going to be and what ended up being in the room was O.J. Simpson memorabilia. But also, there was Joe Montana memorabilia, Duke Schneider, and Pete Rose. When he came in, he just stole everything.

So, the D.A. asked me to serve him with notice to indict him, and he was in jail already. My partner and I had to go down to the jail, and we had to ask the jail to bring him up. He was in jail for one day at this point, and we were made aware that he was causing problems internally for the jail staff because inmates wanted to see him. If he walked down the hallway, people would make their way to the window so that they could get a glimpse of him in shackles.

So, when we went to go serve him with this notice, we did it in a place that was a little bit more secluded. Eddie and I were in the room inside the jail, and we were sitting down at a table, waiting for O.J. Simpson to be brought into us. We heard him coming down the hall because of the ankle chains dragging across the floor as he was walking. I heard the key go into the door, and the corrections officer opened up the door.

O.J. Simpson came in, and he was looking

down at the ground, looking like somebody stole his bag of candy on Halloween. Then he made eye contact with me, and the guy lit up like a long-lost friend and gives me the "Hey Buddy, how you are doing?" expression. Then he sits down and tries to chat us up. But the reality was we were really busy at the time, and I really didn't have time to chat with him. I needed him to sign a form and move on. So, I slid this form in front of him, and he tried to chat me up. Then I told him, "You don't have to sign the form. I'll sign it for you." He says, "okay," signs it, and gives it back to me. After that, I had a ten-minute interaction with him, and when my partner and I were walking out of the jail, I mean, you're holding this document that he just signed, you look down, and there's his famous signature. And you think, wow, that's the signature that starts the whole court process. For all the money he made on signatures, that one put him in.

Q. Where are all those memorabilia now?

A. It went to the California courts, but 98 percent of it went back to the victim from who it was stolen. There were a few items, I think about sixteen, that do legally belong to him.

However, he could not present evidence of receipt of them, so he didn't get them. So, the victim, I think, got back about 600 items.

Another thing that's not talked about that much is there's still property that I was unable to recover. There are still memorabilia. I've recovered some of the Joe Montana stuff and Pete Rose stuff. But there's still Duke Schneider stuff and Pete Rose stuff that's never been recovered.

About two years after the incident, the victim contacted me to let me know that he got the property back. And he sold me three of the pictures that were stolen from the room, which was kind of a nice gesture of him. But he turned around and sold most of those items on eBay and Amazon for about $299 a picture.

Q. This was your first-time meeting O.J. What was the biggest surprise you got?

A. How tall he was. In fairness, I'm a big guy, 6 foot 5 and 300 pounds. I mean, the guy's head is huge. The second thing that caught me off guard was how over-the-top charismatic the man was.

Q. What's the reaction to this case and your book?

A. Most people are unaware of what happened. You know, when Kim Goldman interviewed me last week, those were her thoughts. She didn't know the details of the crime. Obviously, she knew about the conviction and the sentencing. But I don't think most people know what actually happened in that room. Most people just go with what the defense said that he just tried to steal his own property back and got caught.

Q. What did you learn as far as the connection between Kim Goldman and the Vegas case?

A. Simpson made an interesting statement – the crime that happened in Las Vegas was directly connected to the civil settlement with the Goldmans and Browns for the wrongful death of Nicole Brown and Ron Goldman. So, it comes back to trying to hide property or assets from them so that he doesn't actually have to give them money. What was really interesting was that we had a recording of O.J. Simpson after the robbery talking about the property, and he was fully aware that it wasn't the property that he thought it was and that it included sports memorabilia from other players. Once, he tells his co-defendant something along the lines of, "Hey, you guys should keep this stuff because if you don't, it'll go to the Goldmans anyway.

Q. Now, I heard from his lawyer from his murder trial, Shapiro, that the Judge gave O.J. 33 years in this Vegas conviction because one year represented each one million that he owed the Goldmans. Do you believe that?

A. No, but I love the parallel. You know, we look for parallels. And in most things in life, we can find a parallel. So, his prison sentence was 15 to 33 years. But what you'll find is that for every individual crime that he was charged with, there's a sliding scale of what the appropriate sentence is. And when you just simply add up what the jury convicted him of, it just happened to be thirty-three. On that note, if it had been thirty-two years, then Shapiro would have said it was thirty-two years because that was the number of his football jersey. People always try to find a reason for it. It goes back to humanity, the desire not to hold the individual accountable.

Q. What did you think of the parole hearing?

A. He lied.

Q. It was that simple?

A. You know, I've got to tell you it was very frustrating. There was a moment in the hearing when he kind of snapped at the parole board members. In my mind, I had hoped that the parole board members were going to maybe yank O.J.'s chain a little bit and identify how inappropriate that was, but nothing happened. Though I respect our criminal justice system, and I understand that was his time for parole, I just don't think you should be rewarded for being dishonest.

Q. Have you met up with O.J. Simpson or talked with him since the book came out?

A. No. But his lawyer has sent me a couple of messages.

Q. Were they nice?

A. No. His lawyer is an interesting guy. I think he was primarily a personal injury lawyer at first. He has basically accused me of being a liar or misrepresenting him (O.J.). He didn't like how the documentary represented his client. But luckily, I have the facts on my side. I don't have to live in O.J.'s world. I can live in a world of truth.

Q. Now that O.J. is out of prison, aren't you a little bit worried?

A. No. I actually think that he doesn't really care about me. I think he enjoys the attention. I saw this clip of him in a white SUV the night after he was released from prison. The media kind of rushed him at a gas station and started talking to him. O.J. could have ended the conversation by closing the door and leaving the rolled windows. But he didn't. He engaged in conversations. He engaged the reporters. He likes to be in the limelight too much, so I'm not going to be worried about him.

Q. What do you hope people take away from your book?

A. They're going to find out that he didn't steal his own property back and that it was actually a crime regardless of the conspiracy theories or wanting to find out that maybe we prosecuted him for what California didn't do. There is an undeniable connection between the two cases, but it had nothing to do with that.

They'll also get a glimpse into police culture. Sometimes people see law enforcement as being very stoic, and they don't give us a chance to have personalities. So, I think that they'll see some personality in the book. We laugh just like anyone else does.

Listen to the full interview with Andy Caldwell on my website:

https://www.alanrwarren.com/
hom-podcast-episodes/
episode/848f9f49/oj-
simpsons-las-vegas-
conviction-andy-caldwell

References

1. Johnson, Ramon: "Gay Parents—Orenthal James (O.J.) Simpson," *Famous Gay Parents and Their Kids,* May 11, 2016.
2. Toobin, Jeffrey: *The Run of His Life: The People v. O. J. Simpson*, Random House Publishing Group, September 2015, p. 45, ISBN: 978-0-8129-8854-3.
3. Bruce, Aubrey: "Inside Conditions," May 12, 2013.
4. Knapp, Don: "O.J. Simpson Profile: Childhood," *CNN*, June 24, 1995.
5. "A timeline of O.J. Simpson's life," *CNN*.
6. Blevins, David: *The Sports Hall of Fame Encyclopedia: Baseball, Basketball, Football, Hockey, Soccer*, Rowman & Littlefield, 2011, p. 895, ISBN: 978-0810861305.
7. Posnanski, Joe: *Chasing 2,000 in '73*, Archived July 8, 2016, at the Wayback Machine.
8. "O.J. Simpson: Career Capsule," Pro Football Hall of Fame.
9. Goldberg, Haley: "The Hollywood career O.J. Simpson left behind," *Los Angeles Times*, June 12, 2014.
10. O.J. Simpson, *Tonight Show*, 1979, NBC.

11. "History of ABC's Monday Night Football," ESPN, January 15, 2003.

12. Lowry, Brian: "The Saga of O.J.'s Last, Lost Pilot," *Los Angeles Times*, May 8, 2000.

13. Lowry, Brian: "The Saga of O.J.'s Last, Lost Pilot," *Los Angeles Times*, May 8, 2000.

14. Richardson, Lynda: "No Reports of Violence By Simpson's First Wife," *The New York Times*, June 29, 1994.

15. Gibbs, Jewelle Taylor: *Race and Justice: Rodney King and O.J. Simpson in a house divided*, Jossey-Bass, September 4, 1996, ISBN: 978-0-7879-0264-3.

16. Weller, Sheila: "How O.J. and Nicole Brown's Friends Coped with Murder in Their Midst," *Vanity Fair*, June 12, 2014.

17. Gilbert, Geis; Bienen, Leigh B.: *Crimes of the century: from Leopold and Loeb to O.J. Simpson*, Northeastern University Press, 1988, p. 174, ISBN: 978-1-55553-360-1.

18. Mydans, Seth: "The Fugitive: Simpson Is Charged, Chased, Arrested," *The New York Times*, June 18, 1994.

19. Toobin, Jeffrey: "True Grit," *The New Yorker*, p. 28, January 9, 2016.

20. Decker, Cathleen:. "THE TIMES POLL: Most in County Disagree With Simpson Verdicts," *Los Angeles Times*, October 8, 1995.

21. Dershowitz, Alan M.: *America on trial: inside the legal battles that transformed our nation*, Warner Books, May 2004, p. 514, ISBN: 0-446-52058-6.

22. O. J. Simpson prosecutor: "His murder trial ruined my life—but 20 years on I'm back," *The Telegraph*, March 18, 2016.

23. Norman, Bob: "A most-wanted attorney," *Orlando Weekly*, October 5, 2000.

24. "In the Matter of F. Lee Bailey," Mass.gov.

25. Somers, Terri: "F. Lee Bailey Trying To Get $14.5 Million," *Palm Beach Sun Sentinel*, July 24, 2001.

26. "F. Lee Bailey Loses Bid to Practice Law Again," *The Los Angeles Times*, April 12, 2003.

27. Bolino, August C.: *Men of Massachusetts: Bay State Contributors to American Society*, Bloomington, Indiana: iUniverse, 2012. p. 554, ISBN: 978-1-4759-3375-8.

28. "F. Lee Bailey disbarred in Florida," *United Press International*, November 21, 2001.

29. "Thanks to O.J., Bruno Maglis are really big shoes," *CNN*, October 11, 2012.

30. "Fight over money may follow court battle," *Usatoday30usatoday.com.*

31. "Judge Fujisaki was able to keep trial in control," *Usatoday30.usatoday.com.*

32. "O.J. Feels the Heat," *Time*, April 9, 2008.

33. "O. J. part of 'military-style invasion' of hotel room, witness said," *CNN*, November 8, 2007.

34. "O. J. Simpson a Suspect in Casino 'Armed Robbery'," *FOX News*, September 14, 2007.

35. "Police: Simpson cooperating in armed robbery probe," *CNN*, September 14, 2007.

36. "O. J. Simpson held without bail," Crime & courts, *NBC News*, September 17, 2007.

37. Ashley Powers: "4 in Simpson case are given probation - The men who carried handguns into a meeting at a Las Vegas hotel avoid prison, as do two others," *Los Angeles Times*, Associated Press, December 10, 2008.

38. Neal Colgrass: "The Felon Behind O. J.'s Bust Meet Thomas Riccio: Arsonist, prison escapee, stolen goods dealer," *TSG*, December 12, 2008

39. Neal Colgrass: "O.J. Bribed Witness to Alter Testimony: Investigator," *Associated Press*, December 12, 2008.

40. Simpson co-defendant: "Guns were O. J.'s idea," *Associated Press*.

41. "Simpson's Bail Set at $125,000," *Forbes*, September 19, 2007.

42. Scott Glover: "O. J. on Las Vegas hotel incident: 'I've done nothing wrong'," *Los Angeles Times*, September 16, 2007.

43. "Simpson could be charged 'in next few days'," *CNN*, September 17, 2007.

44. Ken Ritter: "New Charges Filed in O. J. Simpson Case," *Associated Press*.

45. "O. J. Simpson was found guilty of all charges in Nevada," *Associated Press*, 4 October 2008.

46. Schilken, Chuck:). "O.J. Simpson granted some parole but will remain behind bars for now," *Los Angeles Times*, July 31, 2013

47. "O.J. Simpson granted parole after serving nine years of armed robbery sentence," *Guardian*, July 20, 2017.

48. Hall, Carla & Krikorian, Greg: "Dreams of Better Days Died That Night: Ronald Goldman: A young man was finding his way through the maze of L.A.," *Los Angeles Times*, July 3, 1994.

49. "On Fatal Night, Nicole Simpson Was Seen With a Man in a Shop," *The New York Times*, August 8, 1994.

50. Dunne, Dominick: "Meet the O.J. Simpson Trial's Supporting Players, from Faye Resnick to Mark Fuhrman," *Vanity Fair*.

51. Margolick, David: "Simpson Guest Testifies Of Strains Before Killings," *The New York Times*, March 23, 1995.

52. Goldman, Ronald: "O.J. Simpson trial: Night of the timeline of the murder," *CNN*, December 11, 2007.

53. People *True Crime Stories: The Trial of O.J. Simpson*, 2019. ISBN: 978-1547847600

54. "First Officer at Scene Ends Long Simpson Testimony," *Los Angeles Times*, February 15, 1995.

55. "Nicole Simpson's Grisly Death Described To Jury," *Chicago Tribune*, June 8, 1995.

56. Margolick, David: "Victims Put Up Long Fight A Witness For Simpson Says," *The New York Times*, August 11, 1995

57. Pemberton, Patrick S.: "Limo driver for O.J. Simpson the night of the killings had a quieter life in Paso after the trial," *San Luis Obispo Tribune*, February 16, 2013

58. Newton, Jim & Hubler, Shawn: "Simpson Held After Wild Chase: He's Charged With Murder of Ex-Wife, Friend," *Los Angeles Times*, June 18, 1994.

59. Winton, Richard: "TV news chopper spotted O.J. Simpson's white Bronco, and the chase was on," *Los Angeles Times*, June 17, 2019.

60. Winton, Richard: "TV news chopper spotted O.J. Simpson's white Bronco, and the chase was on," *Los Angeles Times*, June 17, 2019.

61. *FRONTLINE*: The O.J. Verdict: Interviews: Peter Arenella, *PBS*.

62. "Passenger Describes L.A. Police Beating of Driver, Calls It Racial," *The New York Times*, March 21, 1991.

63. Pemberton, Patrick S.: "Limo driver for O.J. Simpson the night of the killings had a quieter life in Paso after the trial," *San Luis Obispo Tribune*, February 16, 2013.

64. Serrano, Richard A.: "'Bid for Officers' Acquittal Fails: King case: The judge, in rejecting the defense motion, rules that there is sufficient evidence to support a conviction of each defendant in the beating of the motorist," *Los Angeles Times*, March 18, 1992. ISSN 0458-3035.

65. Matiash, Chelsea; Rothman, Lily: "Rodney King Beating at 25: What Happened in Los Angeles," *Time*, March 3, 2016.

66. Cannon, Lou: "Prosecution Rests Case in Rodney King Beating Archived March 5, 2016, at the Wayback Machine," *The Washington Post*, March 16, 1993.

67. The Independent Commission on the Los Angeles Police Department (1991). Report of the Independent Commission on the Los Angeles Police Department (Christopher Commission Report).

68. Wayback Machine The ACLU, "Fighting Police Abuse: A Community Action Manual."

69. Darden, Christopher: *In Contempt*, Graymalkin Media, 2016, ISBN: 978-1631680731.

70. Toobin, Jeffrey: "The Danger of the Bloody-Glove Defense," *The New Yorker*, July 18, 1994, ISSN 0028-792X.

71. Toobin, Jeffrey: *The Run of His Life: The People v. O.J. Simpson*, 2015, ISBN: 978-0812988543.

72. "Some who helped shape the O.J. Simpson case," *USA Today*, January 28, 1997.

About the Author

Alan R. Warren has written several bestselling True Crime books and has been one of the hosts and producers of the popular NBC news talk radio show the *House of Mystery,* which reviews True Crime, History, Science, Religion, Paranormal mysteries that we live with every day.  From a darker, comedic, and logical perspective, he has interviewed guests such as Robert Kennedy Jr., F. Lee Bailey, Aphrodite Jones, Marcia Clark, Nancy Grace, Dan Abrams, and Jesse Ventura. The show is based in Seattle on KKNW 1150 AM and syndicated on the NBC network throughout the United States, including on KCAA 106.5 FM Los Angeles/Riverside/Palm

Springs, as well in Utah, New Mexico, and Arizona.

Read more about Alan on his website:
alanrwarren.com

Also in The House of Mystery Interview Series

The *House of Mystery Radio Show* has been on the air for ten years, broadcasting in over a dozen cities in the U.S. It started as a way to interview guests knowledgeable in many of the world's mysteries involving crime, science, religion, history, paranormal, conspiracies, etc. The *House of Mystery Interview Series* is a curated collection of interviews from the show. Each volume focuses on one of the mysteries, providing the background and reproducing the main points discussed in the interviews. There will be no committed answer at the end, as the Interviews series does not attempt to solve the case. Instead, it provides the most compelling aspects of each theory held by different experts. This series is an excellent reference for researchers and a good overview for those unfamiliar with the case. Online links to the actual interviews are included.

VOLUME 1: JACK THE RIPPER: THE INTERVIEWS

Volume 1 of the Interview Series, "Jack the Ripper," covers the ultimate "who-done-it" mystery of 1888 London. Scotland Yard's "Whitechapel Murder File," in which Jack the Ripper had a starring role, went cold before it could be solved. One hundred thirty-two years later, and the fascination with this cold case mystery continues. Ripperologists passionately debate suspects, opinions, research methods, and theories. Even which murder victims to include in the case is widely debated. Astonishingly, work continues, and today Ripperologists still find new clues that bring us closer to solving the mystery.

the HOUSE OF MYSTERY RADIOSHOW presents

JACK the RIPPER

THE INTERVIEWS: VOLUME 1

ALAN R. WARREN
MICHAEL L. HAWLEY

The mix of credible and diverse thinkers interviewed includes world-renowned historian Neil Storey, the Godfather of Ripper Research, Paul Begg, Ripperologists: Paul Williams, Tom Wescott, Adam Wood, and Steve Blomer. Michael Hawley contributes his unprecedented scientific approach to the case. Suspect Ripperologists Jeff Mudgett, whose great-great-grandfather was serial killer H.H. Holmes, weighs in, as does Russell Edwards, who believes he solved the mystery through DNA.

VOLUME 2: JFK ASSASSINATION: THE INTERVIEWS

Volume 2 of the Interview Series, "JFK Assassination," covers *the* unrivaled historical mystery of historical mysteries. The JFK assassination is the grandfather of all conspiracies in America and arguably where they all started. A highly popular President with movie star looks and charisma, effecting significant changes in society, was brutally cut down in his prime. The official story was that JFK was killed by a sole assassin, Lee Harvey Oswald. However, many conspiracy theorists believe in an assassination plot involving the FBI, CIA, U.S. military, VP LBJ, Cuba's Fidel Castro, Russia's KGB, the Mafia, or some combination of those entities.

The research and interviewing of the JFK assassination experts lasted for over six years. Arguments and counter-arguments from a diverse mix of bestselling authors make for some interesting discussions. And some of the authors interviewed are considered just as controversial as the mystery itself. Most authors focused on who they believe was responsible for the assassination. Others narrowed their focus on certain related aspects, such as the Zapruder film, Nix film, Garrison Tapes, etc. All information collected from each expert adds value to the overall mystery.

VOLUME 3: ZODIAC KILLER: THE INTERVIEWS

Volume 3 of the Interview Series, "Zodiac Killer," covers another serial killer who has stayed in the spotlight for years after their case has gone cold. It's been over 40 years now, and fascination with the Zodiac is still going strong. Experts passionately debate Zodiac suspects, Zodiac"s letters/ciphers, opinions, and theories. Even which murder victims to include in the case is widely debated.

the HOUSE OF MYSTERY RADIOSHOW presents

WANTED

SAN FRANCISCO POLICE DEPARTMENT

ZODIAC KILLER

THE INTERVIEWS: VOLUME 3

ALAN R. WARREN
MICHAEL BUTTERFIELD

The diverse mix of authors interviewed includes cryptologist and cipher expert David Oranchak, authors who propose their suspects are already convicted serial killers, authors who claim the Zodiac was their father, authors who offer new or already considered suspects, and an author who argues the Zodiac killer didn't exist at all and that Zodiac was a hoax.

VOLUME 4: MYSTERIOUS CELEBRITY DEATHS: THE INTERVIEWS

Volume 4 of the Interview Series, "Mysterious Celebrity Deaths," covers interviews relating to the mysterious deaths of the influential rock band Nirvana's frontman Kurt Cobain, the 1960s mega-icon Marilyn Monroe, T.V.'s *Hogan's Heroes* lead actor Bob Crane, the talented and multi-award-winning actress Natalie Wood, and the people's princess, Princess Diana.

VOLUME 5: CONSPIRACY THEORY CULTURE: THE INTERVIEWS

Volume 5 of the *House of Mystery Interviews Series* will focus on theories that go against the scientific facts that we have learned over many generations of the human race. There is something uniquely intriguing about a good conspiracy theory. They tell tales of heroes, villains, and alternative realities.

Conspiracy theories represent secret knowledge: real or not, and there is something very pleasing about having supposed insider knowledge.

Because of their entertainment value, you can find conspiracy theories everywhere. Implausibility doesn't make conspiracy theories less entertaining. What if the moon landing was faked? Who would have been involved? How could they have pulled it off, and why? What if the earth is encapsulated by a celestial lid? What if the infamous leader of the Third Reich escaped Germany? What if President Franklin Roosevelt had allowed the Pearl Harbor attacks to happen?

These are a few of the conspiracy theories discussed in

this volume. As with the others in this series, this book will cover the most popular conspiracies – the ones that have gained lots of ground in the media and on the internet. Some of them even have celebrity followers. During the interviews, guests were shown the utmost respect, as we tried to find out their reasoning for believing what they do and how they developed their beliefs.

VOLUME 6: PARANORMAL & THE OCCULT: THE INTERVIEWS

During the first ten years of the *House of Mystery Radioshow*, the paranormal field was very popular in society, including several television series covering ghost hunting, haunted houses, mediums communicating with the dead, witchcraft, and even Satanism. Spirituality was also discussed since religion is often given the power to either protect or attack one doing the investigation.

In Volume 6 of *The Interviews* series, the shows relating to the Paranormal will be covered in two parts. Part 1 will cover topics relating to Parapsychology, Mediums,

Psychics, and paranormal tools such as Ouija boards and haunted items. Part 2 will cover religion, the occult, and topics such as Near-Death Experiences, Lucid Dreaming, Psychokinesis, as well as paranormal tools such as Astrology, Numerology, and Tarot cards.

The interviews selected for this book were chosen for the guest's believability and knowledge in their area of expertise.

their beliefs.

VOLUME 7: D. B. COOPER: THE INTERVIEWS

This book reviews the D.B. Cooper case. It is divided into five parts. The first part gives the bare facts we know about the hijacking. The second part covers the primary suspects listed according to the FBI, media, or public opinion, supported by the show's best interviews with authors and researchers who covered these suspects. The third part covers the other major suspects popular among the public but not considered Cooper by the FBI or law enforcement authorities. The fourth part covers some of the major suspects who came forward to police and confessed to being D.B.

the HOUSE OF MYSTERY RADIOSHOW presents

D.B. COOPER

THE INTERVIEWS: VOLUME 7

ALAN R. WARREN

Cooper. The last part is dedicated to the wave of copycat hijackings that occurred after the Cooper case. And there were quite a few.